Thru the Turnstile

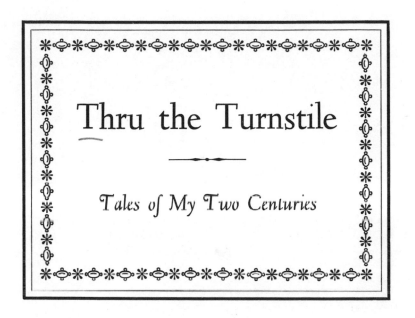

Thru the Turnstile

Tales of My Two Centuries

ALICE CARY WILLIAMS

Illustrated by Samuel H. Bryant

Houghton Mifflin Company Boston

1976

Library of Congress Cataloging in Publication Data

Williams, Alice Cary.
  Thru the turnstile.

  1. Williams, Alice Cary — Biography. 2. Boston —
Social life and customs. 3. Nantucket, Mass. — Social
life and customs. I. Title.
PS3573.I4474Z52   813'.5'4   [B]   76–15977
ISBN 0–395–24404–8

Printed in the United States of America
W 10 9 8 7 6 5 4 3 2 1

FOR MALCOLM
who shared these days

Author's Note

$\mathcal{M}$y publishers have found some minor inaccuracies which I beg will be pardoned due to my age at the time. The stories in themselves are true, though some may belong more to Williams family tradition than to history.

I should also like to take this opportunity to express my gratitude to Mrs. Ruth K. Hapgood, who greatly assisted me in assimilating these tales.

Alice Cary Williams
Nantucket, 1976

Contents

1. Thru the Turnstile   1
2. Oliver Wendell Holmes and His Two Pupils   5
3. My Father   11
4. Julia Ward Howe and I Meet Oscar Wilde   17
5. Boston Blizzards and Obituaries   22
6. Hypnosis   30
7. Out of the Nursery   35
8. The Turn of the Century   42
9. Dissension   47
10. How to Move to Nantucket for the Summer   51
11. My Father and I Go Doctoring   59
12. Without Kody the Prince Family Could Not Function   67
13. The Wild Ponies from Minnesota   74

Contents

14. William Gillette   81
15. An Hour with Grover Cleveland   86
16. Surfside as It Was Then   91
17. Just Bud   95
18. We Move to Boston in the Fall   103
19. The Year of the Spider   108
20. Cleopatra   113
21. The Supernatural Again   119
22. The Hermit   122
23. Professor Pickering   127
24. The County Fair   132
25. Hypnotism Again Attacks Papa   138
26. Under the Harvest Moon   142

Thru the Turnstile

Thru the Turnstile

THIS IS Nantucket Island that I'm walking on, one summer
morning at 5 A.M. It's one of our wet, dense, clinging fogs
that close one within one's self. The scrunch of gravel un-
derfoot as I keep step with the foghorn wailing at regular
intervals alone breaks the silence. A sense of awareness
precluding thought, a tension that makes me look behind
constantly for ghosts or supernatural manifestations grips
me. Alone in a world of nothingness, I keep on, for there
is a purpose to this eerie walk with unreality.

And then, turning a familiar corner, I come upon it. A
house, hung like a phantom house in midair with no foun-
dation visible but its outlines so right! I was born in it
eighty years ago today. I draw closer, becoming apprehensive, for I see a sign above the front door, which depicts
the Jabberwock and reads "Dining from 6 to 9." Close by,
another, "The Mad Hatter," and then I almost stumble

1

over a large white plaster rabbit at my feet. So, that other "Alice" has taken over "my house" and made of it a Restaurant?

I close my eyes. Memories come flooding back to me. I look up at my mother's window and see her sitting by it, hear my father's voice, feel his strong arms, then my brothers teasing me and all of us rollicking about.

How long I wandered down these memory paths I've no idea, but a noise startled me back, and opening my eyes I saw the sun had broken through the fog, making of the phantom house a solid reality on firm foundations, and standing in the doorway the maker of that noise — a man in a white apron, eyeing me with curiosity. Resenting the intrusion of banalities and explanations, I turned away abruptly and left him.

But that night, returning to dine at the now Mad Hatter, I chose the back entrance to the property, where we often used to enter through an old turnstile. It was there, but pointless, for now no fence connected with it. They kept it probably as a relic. Once again the atmosphere was conducive to a pensive mood, for the deepening twilight would soon wrap me in darkness. As I twirled the old friendly turnstile it gave forth its same old squeak. Delighted, I closed my eyes again and slipped down the years once more.

I saw my mother and father standing on the piazza, waiting to welcome Professor William James and Professor Frank Taussig, who were coming to visit us. I was at the turnstile which they would pass through on their way up from the ferry. And here they come, in their funny little stiff straw hats and black alpaca coats. They are carrying valises and, seeing my eyes fastened upon those valises, Professor James laughs.

"Can you wait, Punkin, till we unpack?"

I blush. My parents call and wave and they pass through the turnstile after pinching my ear.

Then suddenly I felt a hand press my arm; startled, I opened my eyes and stared into a pair of anxious-looking blue ones. They belonged to a young man wearing a garish crimson shirt with white dolphins leaping about on it.

"Are you all right, lady?" he asked solicitously. And I realized how absurd I must look to him, an old lady smiling to herself and twirling a turnstile to and fro! Certainly I'd better explain, so I did.

He pressed my arm still harder.

"You knew Professor James and Professor Taussig?" he exclaimed. "I studied them in college and never understood a single word of either. You really knew them?"

"Yes," I laughed. "They were friends of my parents, and so were Julia Ward Howe and Oscar Wilde and Dr. Morton Prince and lots more."

He looked over his shoulder at the friends he was with, then impulsively said to me, "Will you dine with us and talk about these people?"

"Thanks, no," I said, smiling at his eagerness. "I'm tired and am going home to bed, for I've traveled far today."

Again he gripped my arm, and hard.

"Then promise me you'll write down every single thing you remember about these people. It's not fair to not let us all in on it — they were great folk."

"I promise," I laughed. "I think I've always meant to anyway."

And then we parted.

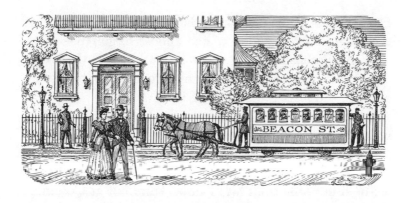

Oliver Wendell Holmes
and His Two Pupils

DR. HOLMES WAS Dr. Prince's and my father's anatomy professor at Harvard and Papa was a worshipful pupil. As Oliver Wendell Holmes died in 1894 when I was two, he was necessarily legendary to me, but my father eulogized him incessantly — particularly one day when I was a formidable twelve years of age, on the occasion when Verney Dahlgren (also about twelve) was wheeled into our driveway in a wheelbarrow with a broken leg. The leg was set and put in a plaster cast while in the same equipage by my Papa, Verney was wheeled home when the job was completed, and in due course he went galloping about with never the vestige of a limp. As we watched the departing wheelbarrow my father said to me, "How many arms and legs, fingers and toes should cry out in gratitude to

5

Dr. Holmes for being made whole again. He taught me everything I know and now he's almost forgotten — a legend. As Professor James said once, 'It is as if the whole of a man's significance had shrunk into the phantom of an attitude — that is the pathos of Death.'"

I think, however, Dr. Holmes lived on considerably in at least these two pupils, Morton Prince and my father. Dr. Prince, in addition to writing some books on mental illness, had a large practice in neurological disorders and lectured not only from his chair at Tufts but at Columbia and further afield. He became a living textbook in a developing field of nervous disorders and psychology.

And my father, besides being dean of Tufts Medical School, pioneered quite extensively in studies of the heart; a treatise written by him was used years after his death as a basic work for students. After his retirement from Tufts my father collaborated with Mr. Forsyth in building the Forsyth Dental Infirmary for Children, the marble structure beside the Boston Museum of Fine Arts. My mother used to say with pride, "We're going to Strasbourg this summer to study the most up-to-date dental infirmary, so I can't play croquet with you!"

I don't think Dr. Holmes became exactly "shrunken into a phantom" — not so long as these two pupils kept his memory fresh.

Morton Prince was the first of the cluster of erudite friends to pass through our symbolic turnstile. He and my father met as seventeen-year-old freshmen entering Harvard in 1870. At first the friendship was one of sheer necessity. Morton Prince was disastrously myopic. My father finally became irritated at apprehensively waiting each

6

morning for the sound of the raised window across the small court that separated their rooms, and the ensuing shout: "Harold, for God's sake come over, or I'll be late as the devil for class!" Or especially, "I hung my underclothes on the chandelier so they'd brush against my face this morning and now they're nowhere to be seen." Or, "I've crawled on my hands and knees over every geographical vestige of this blasted room and there's only one boot in it, I swear."

Easier to room together. This they did and continued to do on through medical school. From the very beginning Morton Prince followed a single track in the early selection of his life's work, psychology. He took anatomy because it was compulsory, but would gladly have scrapped the skeleton, all but the skull, and that he endured only for what it housed. And right at this point he ran astray, for it would be impossible to find a man with a greater devotion and dedication to the study of the skeleton than the small stern professor who gave the course, Dr. Oliver Wendell Holmes. He stamped his foot and roared at Morton Prince with the ferocity of a bantam rooster.

"Your degree in medicine is at stake, Mr. Prince, and I assure you I will give no leeway in the final exams!" he shouted in full class.

"Can't you ride me in on your coattails, Harold? The little pompous goat loves you. I've seen him eyeing you as you chin yourself with one arm in the gymnasium, such envy in his eyes. What a premium he sets on physical strength — because he's so weak and small, I suppose. And pompous! By the way, I heard a good one on him. Seems he was watching the skaters on the Charles; a very small

7

girl came along, they chatted. 'When you go home, little girl,' says he, 'you can tell your parents you were talking to Dr. Oliver Wendell Holmes.' She replies, all innocence, 'And you can tell yours you were talking to little Susan Nichols.' "

"Not funny at all," said my father, trying not to laugh. "My advice to you is, show more respect. *What* a teacher. When he's through with me I can throw away my Gray's *Anatomy*. Do you know that on a bet he assembled the skeleton blindfolded? They piled up the isolated bones, he got everything perfect, complex ear assembly, every inarticulated finger and toe bone, even the teeth. He's a marvel, I tell you. And look at his prolific novels and treatises besides."

"Thanks, I did. I thought a quote might soften up the old geezer, but when I got to 'If I should be the last leaf upon the tree' et cetera, I dozed off in spite of myself. That's one tree, my lad, we could have spared to the woodsman!"

"Well," growled my father, "you'd better bone up on your bones if you want M.D. trailing after them. Personally I'd like to see you get bone conscious, for I'm always dreading to see you come to class just in your 'bone suit' if I'm not around to dress you."

Meanwhile my father's determination to be a surgeon made him avid for anatomy and an avid pupil for Dr. Holmes. Morton Prince marveled at his dedication. Often he leaned against the door of the lecture room, watching, where alone and in the twilight two heads, a gray one and a blond one, bent low over a table full of bones. They murmured in low voices together as they rearticulated the tiny swivel joints of fingers and marveled at the flexibility of the wrist mechanism, in which my father saw the tools of the surgeon. Again they looked in awe at the "lift potential" of shoulder, the "thrust power" in the lower arm. Maybe in picturing the supreme capability of that ancient javelin thrower clad in glowing crimson velvet there was consolation for the weak little professor who would have so coveted that capability.

During their last year in medical school my father married and Morton Prince moved in to live with them. He was getting nervous over the impending examinations and worked hard and long at anatomy, this keeping him many nights late at the medical school. To reward himself after a long "bone-bout" he sometimes had a go in the dissecting room at the cerebellum. A head had been severed from one of the cadavers to facilitate this study and the boys had facetiously called it "Herman." The incident I'm about to tell seems incredible by today's standards and procedures as well as hygienic tolerances, but I can vouch for its truth as told to me.

The fact that Morton Prince, weary one such night and faced with some frustrating snag in his experiments in the left lobe of the brain he was working on, carried Herman home and put him in our icebox, meaning to get up early and continue his experiment, does not surprise me. To him, this head was not a thing of horror, not in his eyes once a living man. Not at all. To Morton Prince it was a material substance opening the door to Science and had no other connotation.

Therefore, next morning he stood in sheer amazement as he looked down on the prostrate form of the cook in a faint and heard with equal wonder my father's tirade. Perhaps his myopia extended to his mind, for he always seemed to see only the certain object at hand and no other aspects at all.

Be that as it may, they both did graduate. Morton Prince squeaked through anatomy with a C, my father with an A.

And then came a three-year separation which took my parents to Europe and to the hospital surgical experience for my father in London and Paris, with a final polishing-off under a world-famous surgeon in Vienna.

[3]

My Father

It HAD ALL BEGUN when a pair of handsome bay cobs had drawn a glistening brougham up to the stately Mt. Vernon Street house and the bridegroom, Harold Williams, handed his bride, Alice Cary, out on to the sidewalk. A battle had been won, and the groom, a stocky, small Welshman, had adorned himself for this event with the full regalia of victory, his patent leather shoes shining, the gold watch chain across his stomach a trifle too large, the red hair redolent with bay rum — quite the dandy, and twenty-two years old.

A victory for him it was, because in 1875 for a trades-man's grandson to aspire to the hand of Grandmama Cary's granddaughter was almost too audacious to consider. Grandmama Cary was the owner of this stately Mt. Vernon Street abode, and a daughter of Robert Treat Paine, a signer of that other declaration of independence.

11

Thru the Turnstile

Alice Cary had lost both parents in infancy and been raised by Grandmama Cary. While rich in blood of the bluest hue, they were poor in purse and Alice had no dot to offer. On the other hand, Grandfather Moses Williams had perhaps the fattest purse in Boston, fed from his sailing ships' cargoes of bourbon and Irish whiskies. Portly of stature, kindly, shrewd and full of wisdom, he looked most favorably upon this alliance.

Seated beside Grandmama Cary on a sofa, he bent most courteously and smilingly toward the tiny, black-eyed, straight-backed lady, who received his gallantry with satisfaction as she moved her fan to and fro, and when able to forget the shade of his blood compared to her own, actually found herself lapsing into quite outrageous enjoyment of his superior conversational attributes.

After all, she reminded herself, apart from the dreadful importing business, Moses Williams was of unblemished reputation and character, respected by all. And her daughter would make a very beautiful bride, she thought complacently — and so my mother was considered then.

So gratified was the grandfather over this alliance that he sent the young pair on a wedding trip across the Isthmus of Panama, where my mother, holding her doll in one arm (she insisted on taking it with her on her honeymoon), leaned from the back platform of the observation car and picked calla lilies as the train jogged slowly along.

Continuing to be pleased, he later financed the trip to Europe for my father's three years of study.

My father did not greatly differ from many men with violent contrasts in their natures. In him was a furious drive that welcomed challenge, even rebuttal — so that men

My Father

called him arbitrary — and a heart so tender he must from sheer shame hide it. The first sometimes clouded his reason by drowning it in emotional thinking; the second he did not always succeed in hiding, as in the case of one small monkey from the lab of the medical school.

Little Alexander-monkey lay dying, fully conscious and not in pain but terrified at what was happening to him. The tiny hand clung to my father's hand, the diminutive round eyes fixed on my father's, pleading for reassurance. Why not the doctor's lethal needle? Punch death into a vein, when such trust existed? He couldn't do that. So together they waited through one night until the life forces slipped away, the little hand loosened, the round small eyes closed. How my father would have cursed had he known a janitor next day gave me the large handkerchief he had laid over Alexander with *H.W.* plainly to be seen in a corner of it.

Now for the trip to Europe. With my mother, one small baby, and another "in transit," they set off in a cattle steamer. Ocean liners, together with other civilized niceties, were unknown in the 1870s. They ran into a terrible Atlantic storm which sent my mother to her berth and slung the cattle about cruelly, those few that didn't die. My father gloried in the storm: lashed with ropes, he rolled about the ship practicing anatomy on sailors' broken bones and helping sling the dead cattle over the rail to the raging waves. My mother in one placid moment said she now understood why the Pilgrims stayed put. What was scalping compared to a return trip? However, one foot on land and the native gaiety of my parents returned. My mother wrote happy letters home to Morton Prince, whom they had left woebegone on the wharf.

Thru the Turnstile

My father benefited greatly in surgical techniques in the London and Paris hospitals and looked forward to Vienna, where he would polish off under that world-famous surgeon. And there at last they journeyed and settled themselves in a tiny apartment.

Vienna was fairyland and they reveled in its glamour. Strauss waltzes played in the outdoor cafés, the beautiful Kaiserin Elizabet rode by their window every morning on horseback and in one ever-treasured moment spied my mother and waved to her. They tasted the famous pastries to the extent the meager exchequer allowed, especially the famous Prinz Regentin Torte, that miraculous achievement of multitudinous layers of chocolate thin as tissue paper.

Then finally the hospital and the meeting with the great Herr Doktor. With his unquestioned skills, the famous surgeon had a "hate complex." He loathed with a deadly loathing all foreigners and especially Americans. Every menial, obnoxious task fell to my father rather than the Austrian students. In the few opportunities allowed him he showed more aptitude and skill than they did, but this only increased his punishments. He took it all light-heartedly enough, believing it to be a universal antipathy to other nationalities, nothing personal to him.

Therefore when one day he was summoned to assist the Herr Doktor in a difficult operation where peritonitis was suspected, my father was flattered and overjoyed. Joshing the other students left disconsolate behind, he strode into the operating room jubilantly. The procedure commenced.

Suddenly a slip of the Herr Doktor's scalpel nicked my father's right hand. Amazed, he glanced up, not believing one so skillful could make much a slip, and was startled at the cold, cruel hatred he saw in those eyes bent upon him for a fleeting moment. Before he recovered, a swab soaked in pus was dropped on the now bleeding cut. Profuse apologies followed from the Herr Doktor. Too profuse.

My father nearly lost his hand with the deadly infection and did not ever regain complete mobility in it. The dream of becoming a surgeon ended!

They returned to America, and under cover and concealment of darkness my father carried both his sick hand and sick heart to his old professor for advice. Dr. Holmes roared and stamped his foot and shouted about "man's inhumanity to man," but he didn't stop there. A letter to the Herr Doktor crossed the Atlantic which, if the dynamite it contained had been activated, would have sunk the ship. The other's anticipated lecture tour in America was canceled; the name Oliver Wendell Holmes carried sufficient weight for that, together with the cutting comment, "We can do this bungling type of surgery ourselves — we do not need instruction from the European capitals in it."

"And now, my lad, you must choose other fields in which to practice and I will help you," he muttered gloomily.

Indeed my father must. With two sons now to support, he cultivated a new field — administrative medicine — and eventually became dean of Tufts Medical School. Dr. Holmes saw to it that he met the personages of Boston's literary society, recommending him to Julia Ward Howe, who immediately made him her physician, and to the many others who later became his friends and came to twirl our turnstile at Nantucket.

That my father was often lonely, with that extreme loneliness we all feel at times amongst people, I know, for

I alone was admitted to his friendship — that place where there are no barriers, all fences are lowered, a place so rarely found in one lifetime. My mother would have been admitted too, were she not too likely to be saddened, she being familiar (as I never was, of course) with the scars of Vienna that never completely healed.

4

Julia Ward Howe and I
Meet Oscar Wilde

"I THINK it's a mistake to take her," said my Mama to my Papa. "She's too young. How do you know she won't scream and disrupt this probably most glamorous occasion of our lives?"

"Bosh, she'll be all right," he ruled.

And so I was taken to Julia Ward Howe's evening soiree where Boston's literati were assembled to meet Oscar Wilde.

The two large drawing rooms were thrown open and a brilliant scene met our eyes as we entered. Beneath the twinkling chandeliers ladies in brocaded gowns of exquisite pastel colors milled about chatting and laughing, their diamond tiaras and necklaces glinting in prismatic radiance. As we made our way through this bevy towards Mrs. Howe,

17

my brother Malcolm and I tightly held one another's hand, neither of us ever having seen such a parade of splendor. Julia Ward Howe in black silk and lace cap sat at one end of the room, surrounded by gentlemen in their somber black with white ties. I made my curtsy to her and she took my hand in both of hers and smiled, her eyes twinkling like a young girl's at my apparent discomfort over the starched piqué garment that I was incarcerated in. Then I was turned loose down amongst the trains and gilt slippers.

Shortly Professor James, seeing my plight, hoisted me to his shoulder and with one finger I gleefully touched a dangle on the chandelier. It was impossible to hear oneself speak, the hum of voices and laughter was deafening to me, but I felt Lord of the Universe on my high perch and no longer afraid.

Passed from shoulder to shoulder, I went from Mr. (later Governor) Draper to Tim Adamowski (first violin in our Symphony Orchestra) to Uncle Mort who nearly dropped me while gesticulating, to Professor Taussig who then rescued me. Mrs. Jack Gardner bewitched me; she wore a scarlet dress cut down to her waist in the back and clashing, I thought, with her red hair and pussy-cat face. She pinched my leg; if I could have reached her finger I'd have bitten it. All my "steeds" seemed to veer her way, I noticed, and enjoy her very lively talk. I much later heard she made no conquest of Oscar Wilde, whom she tried without success to lure to her "palace."

The Adamowski Trio were particular friends of mine: Josef, the first cellist of the Orchestra, his wife Szoumowska, the pianist, and Tim. Szoumowska was enormously fat.

Julia Ward Howe and I Meet Oscar Wilde

She often came to our house for afternoon tea and played sometimes, when Malcolm and I would sit under the piano loving it — all but the price, which was her *wet* kiss.

Margaret Deland was there; she wrote books. She kissed my leg, also a little wetly, but I leaned down and wiped it off when she left, and Governor Draper whose shoulder I was on said "Tut, tut." Everyone seemed very happy, especially Malcolm, who found lovely creamed chicken in the pantry, he told me afterwards, and missed all the dull show ahead. Mama said it was like a royal invitation from the Queen to be invited to Mrs. Howe's.

Suddenly a hush fell over everything, for Mrs. Howe had clapped her hands for silence. The milling crowd moved back against the walls, leaving a clear space before the staircase. I had been put down, so I sat on the floor, below the stairs. It was all so still, not a sound. Then, as I heard a sound above, my heart instinctively began to pound. Carefully raising my eyes, I saw coming down the stairs slowly, slowly, one step, then another, a pair of patent leather shoes with silver buckles, then black stockings and above them green velvet knee breeches, and the knees were bending, bringing the figure down, down, nearer to me. Dare I look higher? If only my heart didn't beat so fast. With an effort I looked up and saw a matching green doublet, a ruffle running down its length, and beside it an arm and hand, a pale white hand which held a lily.

I gasped, I think, as quickly now I looked up into a face which had golden hair surrounding it, falling to the shoulders, and pale blue eyes fastened way off on the ceiling above the guests, and this deathly white face began to speak in a

19

high chanting voice. On it went and on, and when I thought it would never stop it gave a kind of shriek, lowered its eyes, and everyone clapped and shouted "Bravo!"

Then I heard Mrs. Howe's voice, "I don't need to introduce Oscar Wilde." And the figure went towards her, bent and kissed her hand, and the guests began to crowd around him. Malcolm got me and led me to the creamed chicken and I was immersed in it when I again heard Mrs. Howe.

"Will the littlest girl come forward? Mr. Wilde wishes to meet her."

I raised agonized eyes to the kind Irish maid, who wiped the chicken off me and said, "Yes, that's you, sweetheart."

I stood before him and made my curtsy.

"What a ripping little creature," he said, and handed me the lily. Daring to look into his face, and brave now flanked by Mrs. Howe and both my parents, I must say I found it quite human, even kindly, and I liked it, as faces go!

Too bad I never had grandchildren to tell this tale to, for that, I imagine, was why I was taken to see him by my parents!

We all drove home together in a great big double cab and dropped Professor James and Professor Taussig at the Harvard Bridge to take the horsecar to Cambridge. Sleepily I listened to the comments about Mr. Wilde as I held fast to the lily.

"Window dressing," growled Papa.

"Very astute in his summing up of Belle Gardner," said Mama, tongue in cheek.

"A magnetic personality. I met him in the pantry and

carried his suitcase and lily up the back stairs," said mild Professor Taussig.

"I think all of you are damning him with faint praise," said Professor James. "It's a wild, free mind with a thrust into things beautiful, well above the average, in my opinion."

The use of the forbidden word "damn" sparked my sleepy interest into brief attention, I believe, as I dozed off in Papa's lap thereafter.

(Until we sold the Beacon Street house, I could have produced drawings by Mr. Jack Elliott of my appearance at this festivity, even to creamed chicken in my hair. There was also a dried fragment of lily pressed in an old book.)

5

Boston Blizzards and Obituaries

IN THE BLIZZARDS of the nineties, east winds and below-zero temperature kept us in cold storage most of the winter. We unfortunately lived on Beacon Street, in the bend of the river opposite where the Massachusetts Institute of Technology is now, and people had not yet exploded into the Industrial Age with its warm houses.

Our block on Beacon Street beside the Harvard Bridge was one of unending interest to a four-year-old climbing onto a chair to look out upon it. A horsecar went down the center of the street on tracks and stopped whenever anyone wanted to get aboard, going either to Brookline or down Massachusetts Avenue to Boylston Street and the shops. A large single horse jogged slowly along, drawing in winter a closed-in car and in summer a wide-open, delightful, titillating one with seats all across it. The gentlemen welcomed spring and the open car because it did away with eye damage from the ladies' protruding hat pins. Then a man with a barrel, shovel, and broom (Herbie by name), who always waved to me, picked up what Violet the horse left behind her.

An organ grinder and monkey came, and one year Mrs. Bert Bigelow gave me a tiny, squeaky little organ I wore around my neck, and I stood beside him and played it. Papa watched from his office window and it made him cry a little because of little Alexander-monkey.

At dusk the lamplighter came with his long, ignited pole and pushed it up under the globes of the street lamps to light them, and that was getting on to sleepy time and the activities of the street were over for the day.

Our house was built by Arthur Roche and was of yellow brick, one of the innovations he brought home from the Sorbonne. The downstairs hall had a very high mantel with a large blue bowl on it in which Jeremiah, my father's cat, took his afternoon nap on a collection of calling cards and hat pins. Under this was a "Cardinal's chair" which confused Malcolm and me — why was it not at Cardinal O'Connell's up on Bay State Road? — but we supposed it was because Jeremiah needed it for leaping purposes.

The staircase (another Paris innovation) parted at the first landing and went two ways, and there was a huge mirror there. When dinner parties took place (twenty-four persons at a clip sometimes) the ladies on their way up to the library would pause before this mirror for repairs to coiffures and such, to the nervous jitters of Rosa O'Brian, the visiting dinner-party cook, who received all of five dollars for her services and watched her vol-au-vent or soufflé succumb to the delay. Meanwhile Malcolm and I, tucked out of the way on the pantry shelf, awaited tidbits, drooling.

Above the library and parlor floor were two more floors of bedrooms and baths and on top was the final floor with a billiard room and the Nova Scotian servants' bedrooms. Also up there was a true lethal horror, a large skylight extending from top to bottom of the roof, which my father, armed with pail and mop, walked about on and cleaned while my mother hid her face in her pillow and planned her widow's weeds. The glass had no support other than its frames, and if he had fallen through he would have dropped clear down to the first-floor landing. A deadly silence pervaded the whole house when he first stepped onto it until he miraculously stepped off it again.

One of Papa's unkind ideas was a morning bath in ice-cold water. He did it and commanded us to follow suit, but as he slept late after sitting up half the night to read Sir Walter Scott (whom I have since connected with cold baths and heartily dislike), Malcolm and I were able to get away with nice warm baths on the sly.

After a breakfast of mounds of buttered toast, sausages, scrambled eggs, oatmeal and cream, and tankards of milk (never a snitch of fruit, Papa disapproving of it as folderol) we began to wrap ourselves up to face the east wind and go to school. First, for me, a tight woolly undersuit from toe to fingertip; then a waist, drawers, a red petticoat, a white petticoat, guimpe, skirt; over this a black wool covering with drawstrings, a reefer, skating cap, fur mittens, and on below-zero days a veil to temper the cold air to the infant lungs; lastly arctics on feet by now barely ambulatory. To remove these when reaching school left not much time for education, and from sheer exhaustion we also had to eat again before diving into "Gallia est omnis divisa . . ."

A strange sight could often be seen in our house on stormy days: an immobile figure seated on a "humidifier." My father had supplied each hot-air register with one of these angelic contraptions, just fitted to *one* rear end. They merely intensified the heat from the coal furnace. That the registers were two or three hundred yards apart and often on different floors meant that one had to shout if one wished to converse. My mother, who was constantly in a dither over Mrs. Jack Gardner's latest evening dress, once mischievously took this opportunity to excoriate it while my poor father (whose patient Mrs. Gardner was), sitting at a far distance from her, emitted "sssshs" sounding like escaping steam from his humidifier.

In the afternoons at tea-time we went up to our library to warm the front of ourselves before a huge open fire and the inside of ourselves with hot tea and buttered crumpets. The big logs came from Mrs. Arthur Cabot's woods in Ponkapoag, and so were deified, as it were. We *bought* them, but my mother used to add in describing their size, "My cousin Ethel Cunningham married Eliot Cabot," and seemed to get added warmth from the fact. I never understood that, for I went to school with two Cabots and never felt any warmer for it.

We were in the midst of all this comfort one afternoon when the doorbell rang and a stamping and snorting like a cavalry brigade followed in the hall downstairs. Up they came, half frozen and laughing, Aunt Maud, Uncle Mort, and our two Professors James and Taussig. Four abreast they'd braved the storm in their shaggy fur coats, which our Mary had confiscated, and now they barged into several replenishments of hot tea and crumpets, like the wild beasts who'd once inhabited those furry skins.

"We've come primarily to scold you, Harold," said Professor James, settling himself warm and comfortably. "It's just been told me that you took Malcolm through an insane asylum as part of your crazy ideas of child education."

"Yes," put in Aunt Maud, "and Alice says he hasn't got over it yet, cries out in his sleep sometimes still."

My father was silent; he stood before them with his back to the fire as if facing a firing squad.

"His idea," said Uncle Mort, "is to build up immunity to horrors."

"I understand that," said Professor James. "I know that Harold is a worshiper of Pasteur, but I doubt if *he* would concur with shock treatment for a fourteen-year-old as an efficacious serum."

Papa walked to the window and looked out at the storm for a few minutes. Then he came back to his place at the fire. I was surprised that he then spoke so gently.

"My idea is to expose him in small doses to the tragedies in life, so that if some disaster does strike when he's grown, he can cope with it better."

"I hope you don't include Punkin in this horror program," said Professor James, alluding to me.

"*Especially* her," replied my father. "I'll not have her course in life diverted if I can help it."

He walked again to the window turning his back to them. Uncle Mort held up his right hand and pointed to it for

26

Professor James to see and the professor nodded and bowed his head.

Papa came back to the fire and said with attempted gaiety, "What do you say, boys, we work on our obituaries for the *Transcript*? They've been hounding me for Mort's. It's a good day for it."

"Excellent," said Uncle Mort, relieved. "They've been after me too to get yours."

"It is a good idea," said Professor James, though a bit reluctantly, for he hated to give up. "Taussig's been struggling with mine and I'll do his."

Pencils and paper were brought, and save for their scratching and the low hum of Aunt Maud's and my mother's voices, all was quiet. I lay on the floor before the fire, which was burning low; a piece of charred wood fell off, giving out a shower of sparks before falling into ashes. I shuddered. Malcolm, of course, had told me of the dreadful trip Papa had taken him on to the Forest Hills Crematory. He said a narrow iron tray had a lumpy form on it (they were saving the coffin), a cover too, and on the cover a single rose. They slid the tray into a glowing narrow furnace that just fitted it, and clanged the door shut. He heard that clang for days, he told me. But it was the rose that saddened me. Today seemed full of dread somehow. I got up uneasily and saw there were no crumpets left and caught Aunt Maud's twinkling eye.

"I declare I'm hungry again myself, Alice," she laughed, and my mother told me to ring the bell; she was smiling too. Aunt Maud said, "I never get seconds at home without Mother raising her finger and saying teasingly 'Look *carnal* up in the dictionary,' so I did once. 'Dan' calls it 'the opposite of spiritual' but he never lived through Boston winters."

Everyone stopped writing now; twilight was falling and Papa lit the lights and put another Cabot — I mean log — on the fire.

"I can't write Harold's obituary," said Uncle Mort. "Everything interesting is unprintable. Take his world's record in rope climbing at the St. Louis Exposition. Alice says he wore skin-tight pink tights and a peaked hat with a pink ostrich plume trailing down his back. Do you think President Capen of Tufts would appreciate his dean of the Medical School so depicted?

"And just the other day Harold and I were walking past the Charles Street Jail exercise yard and he fussed about the fence being no good and climbed right over it. When he clambered back out a crowd gathered and someone shouted, 'Jail break! Police!' and tried to grab him. I should have left him."

Everyone laughed.

"Well," growled my father, "they are going to change the wall anyway. Don't forget I can downgrade you too, Mort, so people would think you should be restrained."

"Now see here," said Professor James, and he was in earnest. "Mort's work on hysteria and hypnosis is making a decided stir."

"Thanks to me," interrupted Papa. "The crazy girl he just wrote about I sent him as a patient."

"And he cured her," said Professor James sternly, "and you couldn't."

"I wouldn't hypnotize her," said Papa, "if that's what you mean."

"And you don't think her total cure justified it?" Professor James was getting ruffled.

"Certainly not," replied Papa. "When she paid her fee to Mort she also laid a slice of her will on the counter."

Professor James snorted and turned to my mother. I could see he was getting really put out.

"Alice, it's getting late, but can we come again tomorrow — this blizzard is going to last, I'm sure — and have this thing out once and for all?"

"Of course," laughed Mama. "We'd love to have you."

"Yes," agreed Papa, "and view the defeat of William James."

[6]

Hypnosis

THE BLIZZARD did oblige. The friends did reconvene. My father stood back to the fire and opened the argument.

"We were talking about that unfortunate girl, Becky, who at certain times was given to hysteria and irrational behavior to a degree affecting her health, for in them she abandoned herself to tears and grief which she could not control. She had no idea what brought on these attacks, which were followed by severe depression. Nor had I when she came to me as a patient. Nor had Mort at first, to whom I sent her.

"He hypnotized her, probed and questioned her subconscious mind, and at last got at an idea, very clever of him too, I must say. It appeared the girl had been anxious to spend Easter in Rome and persuaded her mother, who was reluctant, to go with her. While in Italy the mother contracted typhoid and died on Easter morning amidst the clanging of every church bell in the city.

"The girl, broken-hearted and guilt-ridden, returned to America and became prone to these abnormal attacks. Mort traced their recurrence to the clanging of church bells. Again under hypnosis he implanted on her subconscious mind the fact that in no way was she responsible for her mother's death, that typhoid might have been contracted in America just as easily. The guilt complex, for that was the cause, was thus removed. Becky was completely cured and became a normal person. Right?"

Both Professor James and Uncle Mort nodded.

"Now," continued my father, "if, as you both seem to agree, the subconscious is a *slave* to hypnotic suggestion, in certain cases couldn't Mort (if he were not Mort) just as easily have told her to revenge herself on me who had not helped her — to seek me out, catch me unawares, draw a knife from her dress, and do me in?"

"In that case," laughed Uncle Mort, "you'd be an accessory as well as the victim for you sent her to me."

"Right," said my father earnestly. "I should have sent her to Mary Baker Eddy. I've sent her lots of neurasthenic idiots and she's performed wonders with them."

"But they are not idiots, Harold, they are mentally ill," said Professor James testily. "And certainly the cure outweighed your Philistine, bigoted notions in Mort's case. Hypnosis is a new, unexplored science, like any other research, subject to possible repellent attempts at experimentation. You don't at the medical school reject biological experiments that grow on horse manure, and bacteria that live on putrefaction. Unfortunately in psychical research we are prohibited from *material* elements and must proceed with what tools we have, but surely progress justifies it."

"No progress justifies weakening the will," growled my father.

Professor James was exasperated. "What does Julia think?" he asked, turning to Aunt Maud.

"I asked her last night, anticipating this impasse," laughed Aunt Maud. "Her answer was, she extolled the research but questioned the practice. At this point you must put Mother in Harold's corner, I think."

My father spoke again.

"For instance, take my hand, boys. I can talk about it now. Even Dr. Holmes agreed with you both, loss of mobility in it was more a psychological idea than actual residual nerve damage. He advocated hypnotism for it by Mort. You'd first have to remove the conviction from my subconscious mind that I would be wrong in accepting hypnosis. What kind of a surgeon, without conviction? No thanks. I'll stay with the biologists and horse manure, and thank God I'm over Mort at least in the Medical School as dean while he's only on the faculty!" He smiled. "Go on with your mediums and telepathy and the rest of the 'bogus' and leave me in peace. You really believe in mediums, both of you?"

"In *strong* mediums, I have found sources of contacted knowledge I find inexplicable — yes." This from Professor James. "One has to plow through endless 'bogus' too, of course."

Papa was a tremendous admirer of Professor James, so he asked diffidently but with curiosity, "Where does this inexplicable knowledge come from? You say the mediums possess it, in your opinion?"

Professor James leaned back in his chair and smiled.

"I don't know, Harold. I have only a *fanciful* idea that appeals to me. Do you all want to hear it?" And he looked around at my mother and Aunt Maud.

"Yes!" There was a chorus of "Yes" from everyone.

"Well," he began, "years ago, suppose in antiquity the universe was in confusion and out of this chaotic condition order finally came. Life, we assume, was in everything, in rocks, in plants, as well as in living organisms, and if we go along with Darwin, evolution formulated these diverse materials into species. Now, suppose fragments, broken-off bits, were left behind, unrelated vagrants as it were, and they, these vagrants, attempted lawlessly to re-enter the world of order and laws, they a disorganized part of the chaotic past.

"They cannot be captured, nor held down, but perhaps, possibly, they may be touched upon by a strong medium, thus accounting for her otherwise inexplicable knowledge."

A long silence followed as the deep, quiet voice ceased. Then after a sigh it continued again.

"It is through following this research in all its phases, *painstakingly*, disqualifying nothing until examined, discarding the fraudulent — that the greatest scientific conquests of the coming generations will be achieved. That is what I believe."

Papa leaned forward, his fingertips together, and he gazed into the fire. There was not a sound in the deep silence save the crackling of the fire. I felt uneasy and tiptoed out of the room and its oppressive quietness.

Thru the Turnstile

(Professor James's comments recorded here were relayed to me years later in substance by my father, as we lay on the bank of the St. Lawrence after a day's canoeing.)

7

Out of the Nursery

ABRAHAM LINCOLN CAME from rugged country and so did Lizzie McCloud, who was his female counterpart in appearance. Coming down to Boston from Halifax, a green girl of eighteen, she landed a job scrubbing floors in the Boston City Hospital. My father, entering the dimly lit hall of that austere institution one day, nearly succumbed to apoplexy at seeing President Lincoln sprawled on the floor, armed with scrub brush and pail. Closer examination, of course, disclosed that he was in a dress, had yellow fuzz on his face and head, and was a woman. Always receptive to new phenomena, my father pursued the acquaintance, after nearly breaking his neck stumbling over the pail on the slippery wet floor and being assisted to his feet by her gigantic hand.

He had her trained as a registered nurse, and when he and my mother left Boston to make the rounds of European hospitals, they took her with them to tend my oldest brother and the next one who was on the way. Harold was two when Ned, the second brother, was born in Vienna, and upon these two boys Lizzie's heart's devotion centered — all of her heart. There was nothing left for Malcolm and me when ten or more years later she was summoned to Nantucket to assist at our births.

Between Malcolm and me there was a stillborn girl, for which I was devoutly thankful when I was told of it, having no desire to have my sole preserve invaded by an older sister, bossy most likely too. She was to have been named for Grandmama Cary, Helen Paine, upon hearing which a Southern friend said, "My, what an awful name, Hell 'n' Pain." It was just as well she didn't make it, from every angle, I decided, for now there was no possibility of my getting that name; it was buried with her, and who knows, they might have had a sudden change of heart and called *her* Alice. Malcolm and I decided we wouldn't have liked her — she was probably one of the sissy kind Mama liked.

I came along six years after Malcolm was born, and particularly incurred Lizzie's disfavor, being a scrawny, miserable thing at birth. Because my mother could not feed me, it seemed I could not settle on any other form of nourishment and was in a fair way of dying. Lizzie, feeling my future hopeless, said to my father one night, "I don't understand, Doctor, when you have those two beautiful, lovely boys, why you bother so over this miserable little scrap of nothing."

"Three boys, Lizzie, don't forget," he snapped.

"Well, yes, three I guess it is, though I do say some things is best forgot. But you can't keep this up, pacing the floor

36

all night and reading them medical books too to find a formula for little Alice. She ain't a-goin' to make it and that's that."

"She is!" he roared. "She must! I want a girl more than anything in the world."

"Well, you've tried everything," she answered complacently, "mare's milk, goat's milk, ewe's milk, even for all I know hen's milk, and there's nothing left."

"By George, Lizzie, you've just given me an idea. A wet nurse. I'll take the early ferry tomorrow and comb Boston till I find one. Mind you, watch little Alice every minute till I get back here to Nantucket with an ample wet nurse. By the way, hens don't give milk," and he winked at her in his new-found relief.

With his usual indefatigable ardor he did find a young Italian woman who had lost her baby, born the same time as me. She could not speak English but through an interpreter he learned that she was willing to go with him, as long as she could be dressed in the accepted garb of a wet nurse, which consisted of a flowing blue cape, a tight cap with ruching on it, and long blue and white ribbons floating out behind, nearly to the ground. This he readily agreed to, waiting patiently till it was paid for and donned, and then together they set off for the island.

On the ferry she reveled in the wind and spray, murmuring ecstatically, "Magnifico!" as her flying cape enveloped the little doctor at her side. But what cared he — willing to face annihilation, practically, if the morsel at home could only be nourished. And as Maria, for that was her name, kept attending apologetically to her leaking bosom, he felt sanguine of success.

Lizzie was infuriated at the good full meals I prospered upon. She sat opposite Maria like a huge stone statue of Lincoln as they took their meals together. Linguistically stymied, Lizzie was certain that not to speak English was perversity on Maria's part. So she yelled at her as if she were deaf. And so frightened by all this was the gentle, sunny-tempered Italian that Papa had Maria eat in the kitchen with the "girls" and kindly James Fox, who took pity on her plight and undertook to teach her English. The lessons took place in his harness room, he pointing out various parts of the harness and giving them their English names, and though I don't suppose Maria meant ever to become a coachman, she warmly appreciated the kind intent.

As Lizzie's venom increased, Papa got nervous, and when finally she hissed one day, "You'll be sorry, Doctor, all them Dagos are handy with a knife. Little Alice may turn out a killer, drinkin' that kinda milk that has no 'human kindness' into it. And what about that wolf mother's children, what she nursed — I left school before I found out what they become — murderers likely and I believe they was both I-talian too, if I'm not mistaken."

Papa laughed. "Romulus and Remus were good men, I believe. We don't really need to have you stay any longer, Lizzie. Little Alice is fine — looks just like Harold," he added mischievously.

That did it. She packed her bag and left, snorting, "You've got your daughter, Doctor, such as she is, but don't think she'll ever equal either of my two lovely boys."

"Three boys, Lizzie, remember?" as he saw her off on the ferry.

In due course Maria, as Malcolm delicately put it, "went

dry," having given me my life, and in tears with much emotion she left us. I kept no memory of her.

"I think, if you'll excuse me now, I'd like to go to bed." Malcolm, age six, sat opposite the new nurse Kate, who, having cached me for the night, had come to undress him. Knees tight together, the long-fingered little hands clasped and resting upon them, he turned troubled large dark eyes upon her face. Offer to "strip" this dignified little person she could not bring herself to do — so, confused, she arose, walked to the door, and wished him a good night.

It was Kate's routine to turn down the beds before supper. Papa had taken Malcolm fishing one day the following summer with a jolly party of older men and in their joking and hilarity forgot to offer him at noon the relief of the chemical toilet in the boat's cabin. Kate on her evening rounds saw him, clad in a clean little suit, hanging all his clothes of the day on chairs by the window with great care, to dry.

"Did you enjoy your day fishing?" she asked, puzzled.

"Not at all," he answered. "I sat all day in a martyrdom of wet."

Aloof, a loner, this tall, dark-haired, slender child moved like a stranger amongst the family of redheads at first, until I grew big enough to cope with things. His bureau drawers were symmetrical, the little rows of shoes in his closet precise. And then finally I tumbled rollickingly into his reserves, dispersed and scattered the pattern of order, brought amazement and some merriment into the serious dark eyes, and we became a solid, inseparable phalanx of two.

My mother, whom he resembled in appearance and in

sensitivity, had become so accustomed to suppressing the latter amidst us rough and ready "Welshmen" that she found it impossible to recall that sensitivity to fit his needs. And so, he and I faced the older brothers and the world in our solid formation.

As we grew older, the long-fingered little hands became able to stretch two notes over an octave, and on winter evenings at twilight when no one was about to jeer, he went to the piano (me under it) and improvised Debussy-like chords, some discordant, troubled, seeking — many evolving into beautiful modulations and always all of them ending in the minor. Yet he couldn't read a note, never heard of Debussy.

In the summers we two rode over the moors on our ponies, swam, fished, sailed, and dreamed. Papa, to whom Malcolm always remained an enigma, bought him a twenty-two-foot knockabout one year. Masculine superiority required me to polish the one small brass cleat while he sat on a deck chair in a yachting cap, smoking a chocolate cigar — this act put on because moored near us in the harbor J. P. Morgan sat aboard the *Corsair* smoking his cigar.

When I was eighteen, Maria was shown unannounced into our library in Boston one afternoon, gazed at me a moment, then rushed towards me and clasped me in her arms. Outwardly I knew this was a stranger hugging me — but I was not either alarmed or repelled, and inexplicably, though still not knowing who she was, I hugged her too and felt a surge of warm affection. There is a tie, I vouch for it. Perhaps the lethal effects are yet to come; murderous inclinations towards members of the human race I have felt, yes, but not sufficient to seize the knife! We had a lovely visit.

Another visit took me on a motor trip one year through Nova Scotia, and at the earnest entreaties of Harold and Ned I promised to visit Lizzie McCloud and report to them about her. After a cool reception (which I shared) I told her how Harold had won a case before the United States Supreme Court and how Papa was proud of it. Leading me to her bedroom, she took from her bureau a picture of an infant in a long dress, drooling, and said with tears in her eyes, "Just to look at him here, the blessed, you could tell he could do it." After a long sigh she murmured, "I'll never be able to forgive the doctor for having that darling Ned be born in Vienna, so he never can be President."

8

The Turn of the Century

THIS WAS to be my second experience of "night life." It was December 31, 1899. Differing from the last time, when I met Oscar Wilde in the dark hours of night, this was to witness the birth of a Century. It would be even more trying too, because the creamed chicken preceded it this time, thus robbing a probably boring night of its needed climax. Mary had snitched for us this delicacy from the downstairs dinner party vol-au-vent and we were gorging, Malcolm and I, at an early nursery supper.

"Funny thing," he remarked, "it's 1899 now and in a few hours it'll be 1900."

"How's that?" I asked indifferently.

"I don't know exactly," he replied, "but I think it has something to do with that Isaac bird on the front of the Technology Building; anyway we'll know soon, for we have to go at midnight and see it happen."

The Turn of the Century

"He's no bird, he's Sir Isaac Newton," I growled. "I heard Professor James call him that."

After what seemed only a few minutes' sleep, I was pulled out of bed, cross as a bear, rolled in layers of clothing and my "animal bonnet" and set in a big cab with Uncle Mort, Malcolm, and my parents. We could only drive as far as Charles Street, for Beacon Hill was swarming with pedestrians, all walking up towards the State House. We joined them. The hill was fearfully slippery and it was bitter cold.

I hated everything, especially that hill, where I'd so often seen the poor coal-wagon horses struggling to keep on their feet. They didn't always either, broke a leg sometimes, and their cruel drivers beat them when they wouldn't even try to get up after they fell down.

We passed the Somerset Club, where a warm old gentleman stood in a lighted window looking down on us.

"Easier to get into the Charles Street Jail, climb over the wall anyway as you did, than to get into the Somerset Club," said Uncle Mort, spying the old gentleman and speaking ruefully. "— and far less expensive," and he chuckled.

Finally we reached the top. The golden dome was brilliant on the State House. I wondered if our "gas lighter man" fixed it up; I was always running to a window facing Beacon Street to wait and see him light the street lights with his long pole lighter when it was getting dark. There were flickering candles in lots of windows and pretty good starlight over head, as I remember.

We were by now getting fearfully jostled and squeezed — a bit frightening on the whole. I heard Papa, whose hand I held, growling; then he said to a man, "You here, Ginn?" and I knew then why he growled. This person who I think published textbooks was one of Papa's pet hates, and here he was squashed in his arms practically. Then I spied a friend of mine, Old Isaac, the rags and bottles man. He often came to our back door for rags, and sometimes he brought me a red banana from the United Fruit stall in the Faneuil Hall Market. He had his bell now, not of course his two-wheeled cart.

"Hello, Isaac," I said, pulling his coat, and then he and Papa began to chat. Papa agreed to Isaac putting me up on his shoulder for he was fearfully tall and I was getting trampled on. Then I saw Mama clearly; she was talking to Major Higginson. Uncle Mort and Malcolm were with her; they'd gotten a little separated from us. She gave me a rather amazed look and flashed her eyes angrily at Papa, who chuckled.

Isaac gave me his bell to hold and taking out an old watch from his garment somewhere, said to Papa, "Just a few seconds now and she'll be able to make as much noise as the rest of 'em." And in a few seconds I knew what he meant.

Suddenly, there was such a tremendous blast of noise as I never had heard in all my life. Every church bell clanged in each belfry over the city. Boats blew their shrill whistles from the harbor. The crowds of milling people all around us shouted and yelled till they were hoarse. And from the North End the Italians came flocking out of their tenements beating pots and pans. And I on my high perch rang Isaac's bell with all my might. It was deafening while it lasted — which wasn't awfully long — and we began to move on down the hill again when it was over.

The Turn of the Century

"I'll keep her on my shoulder, Doc. It's so slippery, if she falls she's likely to get walked on already yet. Savvy?"

"Right," said Papa, who was greatly enjoying Mama's waspish glances, as she remained gladly separated from us in her previous entourage. Isaac began to talk to Papa very earnestly as they moved cautiously down the icy hill.

"Celebratin' goin' on in every village and town over the whole world tonight, my Budapest too, rich and poor, high 'uns and low 'uns rubbin' shoulders all together. Takes, seems like, a great big happenin' like this to suck folks up outa their own selves and little businesses into it. An' look it, Doc, every one o' us is movin' in the same direction, maybe squeezin' and jostlin' one another, but not warrin' nor fightin'. So a feller falls, another feller helps him up on his feet again. T'would be kinda nice if it stayed that-a-way but t'won't, 'cause it's agin human nature."

"How long have you been in America, Isaac?" asked Papa, curious now.

"Oh, goin' on four carts worth, I'm on the fourth cart now, wore out three."

"You've learned a lot," said Papa.

"Naw, I ain't learned nothin' book-ways but I've done a pile o' thinkin'. I've a son who's smart though. Says he'll be Regent o' Harvard College some day," and Isaac chuckled. "He may be sometime, you know it, Doc, now that this less choosy century's got a-goin'."

"He may indeed," replied Papa. "You've built the foundations for him and others, all of you immigrants. Your part won't show — seems unfair, for he and his kind could never rise but for you."

45

"Ain't unfair, Doc. We ain't fit to show. If I ever had a doubt of it, which I ain't had, I can see it tonight in your lady's eyes."

"You don't see it in mine, Isaac. She just doesn't know you as I do. If I can ever be of any help to your son tell him to look me up at the Tufts Medical School — I work there. And thank you for your shoulder and our conversation. Good night."

(Isaac's descendant did become Regent — that is, an Overseer — of Harvard. Also he collected a famous lot of paintings which I saw once in his home when visiting him.)

[9]

Dissension

SCHOOL DAYS BEGAN very badly for me. I was now eight years old, the age, according to my father's somewhat unusual ideas, at which babyhood ceased and it was time to plan a career.

Enrolled at the baby school that winter, I guess I felt an inferiority complex, my classmates being Governor-to-be Leverett Saltonstall, Counselor Susan Brandeis, archaeologist Philip Means and Paul Revere's granddaughter Susan. Anyway the first act of my career was to get myself expelled from this prestigious institution. Despite the tremendous prestige this gave me amongst my associates, I carried the note from the principal around in my pocket several days before presenting it to my parents.

I chose one afternoon when our friends were all gathered for tea in the library, before a roaring fire as usual. Papa's face flushed as he read portions of the note aloud.

47

"The woman's a fool. Listen to this. 'As one educator to another' — the impudence! And here too: 'inciting to riot.' You did quite right, baby," turning to me, "to lock the creature in the closet. I wouldn't have you under the wing of such an ass another day. You can find yourself another school; that one certainly is no good."

A bleat from Professor James, who leaped clear out of his chair.

"Winged ass indeed! Have you lost your senses, Harold? Punkin, who can't even read properly without her finger, is to find herself another school? And you condone the locking in the closet of this poor suffocating female?"

"Don't get so excited, James," said Papa mildly. "She's quite able to find a school for herself. I'm too busy now anyway with the midyear exams. As for the 'suffocating female,' she was in no danger, probably did her good."

"Come, Taussig, let's go." Professor James was terribly upset. "I can't trust myself another minute. As for your being insulted at being classed with her as an 'educator,' I think *she* is the one who should be. Really, at times, Harold, it strikes me that brainwise, pink tights and ostrich plumes set you off at your true value." Bowing perfunctorily to Mama and Aunt Maud, they hurried downstairs and we heard the front door slam. The others left behind burst into gales of laughter.

I had no trouble finding another school. Wandering aimlessly about the streets one day, I saw a lot of girls playing on the sidewalk in front of a school at their recess and when the bell rang I went in with them, hung my reefer with theirs in the closet, and followed them into the classroom. At an empty desk I sat down.

Dissension

Miss Mary Haskell (bless her memory) looked at me somewhat surprised, looked again, and then for the next nine years continued to look at and through me.

"A most intelligent, charming woman," said Papa.

"A very nice school," said Mama. "Mrs. Richard Cabot gives a course there in logic and another one in ethics, you know, Ella Lyman Cabot." Mama here ran the words over her tongue like candy. "She's so delightful."

"Can't be much of a course," said Papa snappishly, showing how badly in need he was of the former course himself. "Richard Cabot has a head shaped exactly like an egg." I remembered then that Dr. Cabot was another of my fiery father's unchosen ones, some civic war I believe over district nursing.

But it did not end here. Professor James came back one afternoon, making it quite clear it was only "to inquire over Punkin's scholastic matters."

"Reading without her finger and even now in long division," said Papa mildly.

"Papa." I was in his lap in one of those delightful confidential moods, inspired by an extra bar of popcorn. "Professor James is sometimes 'solemncholy,' isn't he?"

Papa laughed. "Sometimes short on humor, possibly. Why?"

"He's so hot and bothered over whether I read with or without my finger. What the hell difference does it make?"

"Sssh!" said Papa. "No stable talk around Mama. To answer your question, baby, Professor James has read so long without his finger and read so much and knows more than anyone we know, that he's sort of lost touch with everything else."

I sighed. "I love him," I said finally. "Why *do* I love him, Papa?" Papa laughed. "Perhaps because:

What made the lamb love Mary so?
For Mary loved the lamb you know!

"But Professor James is very put out with me," he went on. "He'll get over it in time — but it takes him time."

10

How to Move to Nantucket
for the Summer

AT LAST. Two cabfuls of us drive to the South Station and begin the trek to Nantucket. Uncle Mort is with us this time. He made his New Year's resolution that bitter cold night on Beacon Hill, when on December 31 or January 1 the centuries jumped about: "I'm not happy without you, Harold, you old dog," he had said, "so I'm moving the family from Nahant and am determined to buy a house at Nantucket." Now he was about to look for one.

At the station platform we met our James Fox. He looked like a wigwam, for he was draped in horse blankets, only his grin visible.

"The horses is all loaded in the baggage car, Doctor, I just come to tell you. I darsn't leave these good blankets for them foreign-raised train men to steal, hard enough time I had beggin' for heavy blankets," and he winked at Papa.

But neither parent was in a joking mood. Once we were in the stiff, too short, red plush train seats I examined my mother and father more closely. They had wild looks on their faces and seemed about ready to fall apart. Mama's hat had listed badly and was now teetering over one eye. Papa's straw hat sprouted with all our tickets stuck in its hatband. We had long yellow tickets in those days for the dual purpose of train and ferry, and they waved like sheaves of wheat on Papa's hat.

Suddenly he made a frantic turn to speak to Cassie, who was in the seat behind him and Mama.

"The cats, Cassie! I clean forgot about them. Are they quiet in their law-bags?"

"Yes, sir, quiet as mice," replied Cassie soothingly, even while choosing the least soothing simile. "See, Doctor, Clo is with Winnie across the aisle and Latch with Mary, while Atro is here with me and Alice holds Pansy-Pussy."

"Thank God," muttered Papa fervently.

"Harold, if I may make so bold, what is a cat doing in a law-bag?" asked Uncle Mort.

"Oh, that," Papa replied solemnly, for this was no time for jest. "Moses and Charlie carry those green baize law-bags to their offices every day, you know; all lawyers use them for legal papers they bring home at night to work on. If you pass the bar examinations you have to get a green bag. They save them for me. They have a drawstring and make perfect traveling cat bags."

Uncle Mort kept a straight face to accommodate the

general atmosphere of tension, but he was curious enough to continue questioning.

"Why are you so upset, old man?" he asked. "As if the gong of doom were about to sound."

"I am, and it is," growled Papa. "You've no idea what these moves to Nantucket take out of Alice and me each year, Mort. Last year, for example, it was a new horse I'd bought at an auction. He would not get into the baggage car until I lit a little fire of newspapers under him, and then he gave a thundering leap in, landing on a blasted parrot. I had a devil of a row with the station authorities over the fire and a worse one with the old woman who owned the parrot."

"Did the horse kill him?" asked Uncle Mort, his face stiff with the effort not to smile.

"Of course not," acidly, "only deranged him slightly. James said he never heard such obscenities as he got off, especially at stations for the amazed pedestrians to enjoy and investigate.

"That was last year," went on Papa gloomily. "The year before, Malcolm got out at Falmouth to be sick and got left behind somehow. Alice nearly went out of her mind and James and I had to unload the horses at Woods Hole, harness them to the new wagon, and drive back after him. He was running up the track crying and of course we missed the ferry."

The train started with a terrific jerk, finishing Mama's hat as well as Uncle Mort's pince-nez, which flew away. Papa crawled all over the aisle looking for them, muttering reminiscences of the parrot's words; he couldn't find them, but the conductor's foot did and the pince-nez perished with a scrunching sound.

"Oh, Lord," groaned Papa, as the handle-bar-mustachioed conductor went into shock. "Now I'll have to lead you around the island, Mort, or else put blue glasses on you, a tin cup in your hand, and leave you on the wharf. You can't see a blasted thing, can you?"

But Mort was the boy of the hour. From each pocket he produced an eyeglass case and warbled sweetly, "Four more, all made up, are on call at Lloyd's."

"Thank God," said Papa. "I'd never have credited you with that much foresight."

Still on his knees, Papa was being plucked of his wheat sheaves by the shattered conductor, who counted as he plucked. "That's right, Doctor," he said, allowing my father to arise, "one for James in the baggage car and the little girl doesn't need one. Sorry, Dr. Prince, I'm real, real sorry 'bout your eyeglasses. I'd kinda think you'd favor the ear kind, they anchor better," and he moved on up the aisle.

A few passengers tried to hide their smiles as Papa stiffly took his seat, thoroughly annoyed over this clownish role Uncle Mort had forced him to play.

We reached Woods Hole at last and left the train. Fortunately the ferry was there, lashed firmly to the wharf. Had it not been or should it decide not to stay lashed (which it was temperamental enough to do even without fog) we would be really in a "Hole." Only one drummers' hotel, permanently reeking of cabbage — no eat house — no adequate stable for the "parrot horse" should he decide he didn't like its listing old stalls.

But the gods were with us. It was there. The ferry, a side-wheeler, consisted of a hold, one deck with staterooms, a third deck for hurricanes (and so called the "hurricane deck").

The horses went into the hold and were tied to rings on the wall amidst a conglomeration of crates of groceries and trunks, which unfortunately they frequently defiled, becoming nervous at keeping their footing as the ship rolled. But we expected this.

The girls and Mama flew to their staterooms and threw themselves on the beds therein, while Papa and Uncle Mort, Malcolm and I went up on the hurricane deck and slid up and down it with the motion, in little camp chairs, to my brother's and my delight.

As we headed out to the open sea, my heart nearly burst with joy at the thought of the long summer ahead on my beloved island. The ferry rolled a lot — Captain Barker told Papa one sidewheel was patched and heavier than the other. Soon we heard the bells of the *Cross Rip* lightship; as we neared it the nine men stationed on it crowded to its rails. They were government-employed on it for a four-month completely isolated stretch — no communication whatever, save to signal the passing ferry with a flag or, weather permitting, a megaphone.

Our crew tossed them newspapers — sometimes reaching target, more often falling in the sea. Papa was their doctor, on a government assignment.

"They're a rough lot," he told Uncle Mort, "drunks wanting to dry out, law escapees, waterfront bums wanting to pick up a few dollars."

"Do you get many calls?" asked Uncle Mort.

"Not many. They fight quite a lot, nothing to do but keep the place shipshape, put out the lanterns at night, otherwise, fish and play cards."

"The bells constantly ringing could be a mental hazard," said Uncle Mort.

"They're not that sensitive," laughed Papa. "Otherwise they couldn't stand bobbing up and down there day in, day out."

Who'll spy the outline of land first, the water tower, the Unitarian church steeple? Me, because my heart beat hardest for a sight of them.

And then came the hawsers being thrown onto the wharf and tied to the great mildewed posts, the gangplank thrown over, and — we had arrived.

Papa went ashore first. He had to shoulder his way through the shouting carriage drivers, who held out eager arms and hands to attract the travelers to the special brand of hostelry they represented. Deafening cries as Papa struggled smiling past them. "Springfield House!" "Point Breeze!" "Welcome back, Doc!" "Nesbitt House!" "Sea Cliff Inn!" "Family all well?"

He was pushing for Tom Hoy, who, confident, relaxed, smiling broadly, was waiting with his carriage and two others manned by little Tom Hoys. Confident because he knew we were his; hadn't Papa relieved him last summer of portions of his anatomy and promised him this business?

We drive up to the house. Our house. I'd forgotten how high up off the ground it stood. Of course it had to be on stilts practically because each fall when the Line Storm struck, the ocean overflowed into its nether regions. I smiled to myself as I recalled Mama exploding, for the laundry was down below and she always blamed Papa.

"How can I keep house in this soggy mess, Papa?" she'd snort. "Do you expect Cassie to swim to and fro between the wash tubs and the ironing board?"

And he'd pat her on the shoulder and say "Now, now, Mama, perhaps we won't have another storm like this."

Up the piazza steps and into the front hall. A pungent smell of peat greets us and a glow from the fireplaces, for June nights are chilly. There on the hall table sit our candlesticks waiting to be carried up to bed. Each one painted the color of its owner's bedroom, each has its little pointed snuffer and taper. Uncle Mort has to be watched; he's so careless about these matters that once he got the wrong color and got in the wrong bed.

I take my blue candle and start for bed, tired from excitement and happiness. I miss Professor James as I look at his candle; I hope he'll come again soon. My room is the littlest in the house, comfortably next to Papa's room. Once in bed I try to stay awake. The scent of new-mown hay from the freshly cut field next door comes in my window, as does the sound of the far-off bell buoy's clanging. Tomorrow will come freedom. I'll be galloping over the moors on Shimmo, feet braced in the stirrups, sitting back easily in the saddle, hair blowing out behind in the wind. Then at noon, stretched out full length on the sweet fern resting, Shimmo near by munching oats from her nosebag.

Alone — no one within miles of us — and silence, save for bees buzzing around about their business affairs and the far-off boom of the breakers on some distant beach.

Thru the Turnstile

Clouds float lazily overhead in the azure sky. Sweet perfume of rosa rugosa and wild sweet peas mingled with the spicy scent of blueberry and huckleberry bushes Shimmo crushes with her hooves. Lying there so, does a child think? Probably not, but absorb? Perhaps, and dream.

If not, why do so many old people return to their homeland? All over the world this happens. Is it merely to rest or is it perhaps to repair the shattered dreams with unshatterable memories, and they choose these places where the dreams were born? Some doubtless find those dreams again, receptive to repair, discovering scar tissue can be stronger than the tissue was before.

11

My Father and I Go Doctoring

ALMOST AT ONCE my father plunged into much work and couldn't give time to Uncle Mort for house hunting. Mrs. Captain Murray had a growling appendix that filled Papa with apprehension. Many people too had saved up their aches and pains, awaiting his arrival on-island. Uncle Mort couldn't do it alone — so he rented for the summer a house whose principal asset seemed to be its proximity to ours; then he went back to Nahant to collect his belongings and his family.

"Thunderation," said Papa to him, "now with you gone I'm on a raft alone in case I have to operate. Dr. Burrage, a vacationing surgeon, is not due for a month and Jack is taking his pre-med exams off-island."

"Well, there's no telling when Mrs. Captain Murray's appendix will make up its mind," said Uncle Mort. "Not much sense my waiting."

"No, you're right. Go ahead and get back as soon as you can. I've never done abdominal surgery — I don't know if this hand will hold up, not go numb on me."

"You'll come through if you have to — you always do," said Uncle Mort consolingly, and left for Nahant the next day.

In the middle of the next night, the familiar ghostly shriek came reverberating through the house. Someone had blown into the ox-horn nailed by the front door to summon the doctor. A spasm of apprehension went through me. I lay still in bed listening to Papa going to his window and calling out in a muffled though anxious voice.

"Yes, who is it?"

Then I heard a strange voice, very deep, very low, very quiet. "It's Mrs. Captain Murray, Dr. Williams, and you'd better make haste."

"Who are you?" cried Papa. "Can we give you a lift?" But a horse's hooves were already going out over our driveway and there was no reply.

As I lay wondering who that could be, I heard my parents' mumbling voices in the hall. They were arguing. Finally my door was opened, Papa stood there with his candle; he was leaning over lighting mine.

"Get up and dress, baby, quickly. You have to go with me."

"You really mean it, Papa? I think you're crazy," said Mama, right behind him in her nightie and pigtail.

"I've no choice, Alice. No one in this house can stand blood besides her. She's seen one operation. I've no time to hunt up anyone on the island and no assurance they'd do any better. Besides I may not have to operate — that

stranger may have been exaggerating. I wonder who in
the devil he was."

My father was terribly agitated, I could feel. He seized
his medicine bag and we hurried to the barn where Jet, the
night horse, was always harnessed and tied ready for her
possible services. He lit the lantern on the dashboard,
opened the barn doors, we jumped into the runabout, and
Jet clattered out and off.

Over the cobblestones her hooves rang out as we passed
through the village. All the houses were dark, the light
from our lantern falling on the black windows, rather
menacing-looking. I nestled closer to Papa; it was very,
very dark. He put his spare arm around me but didn't
speak. Jet stretched her muscles into a tremendous stride
and, once on the dirt road, bits of sand and gravel flew up
from her flying hooves over the dashboard and stung our
faces.

"Take the reins, baby, and drive; you know the turnoff
to Captain Murray's."

I did, and noticed Papa working his fingers in and out
on that right hand and rubbing it. This he did steadily. I
felt his nervousness. Glancing back I noticed another lantern following us way, way off and told Papa.

"Blast him," he growled. "Must be Silas the undertaker.
He must have heard Jet's hooves on the cobblestones and
hustled after us. He's heard rumors all over the village
how bad Mrs. Murray is, I suppose. I wish to thunder he
wouldn't follow me every time there's a serious illness —
it's unnerving." And he rubbed his hand more vigorously.

We arrived. I jumped out and took out from the back
of our gig the heavy stone with the ring in it. It had a long

strap attached, to which I tied Jet. Papa had leaped out, seized his medicine bag, and hurried towards the house where he met Captain Murray at the door, shaking and wringing his hands.

"Thank God, you're here! How did you know to come? She's terrible bad, Doc, a-ravin' and a-tossin'."

Papa pushed past him and went into the bedroom. I followed. A big woman lay on the bed, her face fiery red and sweating, her fingers twisting the sheets as she turned her head to and fro on the pillow. Papa put his hand on her forehead.

"Probably 104 degrees. I can't run the risk of taking her temperature though, she'd bite the thermometer, raving as she is, and I dare not turn her over.

"We've got to operate, Murray. Put on the teakettle and clear the kitchen table."

"Pull that lobster pot, you doggone squirt," raved Mrs. Captain Murray. "It hurts my stomach somethin' awful pullin' on it." Her words thick, garbled — ghostly.

Captain Murray stood looking at her, tears in his eyes and wringing his hands, so I galloped to the kitchen, stirred up the fire and filled the teakettle, seeing he wasn't going to do anything. Papa was rummaging in his medicine bag.

"Put a clean sheet on the kitchen table," he snapped, looking up at me after glancing sharply at Captain Murray.

Then he wheeled around and faced Captain Murray.

"God damn you, man, pull yourself together. We, you and I, have to carry her and put her on the kitchen table and without the least jarring. Or," and his eyes flashed, "do you want me to call in Silas the undertaker, who's outside right now?"

My Father and I Go Doctoring

I had never heard Papa swear before in my whole life, nor I guess had Captain Murray, for he seemed so startled he straightened up and approached the bed.

Like eggs they carried and laid her on the kitchen table. My kettle was boiling and I'd found a basin. Into it we poured the water, instruments, and lots of carbolic acid. Onto a towel went a big splash of ether, which Papa laid over the woman's gaping mouth and her nose. She struggled for a few choking gasps, then came a blessed respite of quiet, except for the heavy breathing.

I felt sorry for Papa, working his fingers in and out of the painfully hot water.

"Hold that towel over her face, baby," he ordered, "and when I tell you, pour more ether on it carefully."

Ether was like gold, I knew, and we had only six cans for emergencies for the entire summer.

The room was stuffy, a fly buzzed on the window pane. Captain Murray had collapsed again; he sat by the stove, his face in his hands. I heard the scalpel cut through hide. I smelled hot blood. With my spare hand I reached for the edge of the table and squeezed it hard. I glanced angrily at the fly and saw the window was rocking to and fro.

"More ether," snapped Papa, and I took the can in both hands. "Whoa," he called, "that's enough. Get that other basin, find the alcohol in my bag and pour some in, then come here."

I guided myself by sliding my hand along the wall, and complied.

"Now hold it right over the open cut — steady." He was so tense, his jaw so tight, the words were almost indistinguishable. I managed to do it. Very gingerly, again as

63

if it were thin-shelled eggs he was afraid of breaking, he lifted something out of Mrs. Captain Murray's abdomen. I dared not look at it, except sideways, as he gently laid it in the basin.

"Thank God!" he muttered, and seemed all of a sudden to slump. "We got it, baby. The water's not too hot for your hand now in the instrument bowl, so you can thread me that needle — it's in the disinfectant — with the catgut."

I crept to the sink and laid down my basin with the thing in it. Perhaps I'll feel better if I kill that fly, I thought, and did I give him a mighty swat with a dish towel.

After a bit of doing I got the catgut into the eye of the needle and Papa sewed her up and bandaged her. Captain Murray still sat with his head in his hands, only now he was whimpering sort of.

Papa went over to him and shook him.

"Get up, Murray, I want her back in bed. We got the appendix — it didn't break. There's no peritonitis, so she has a chance."

"What's that, Doc?" mumbled Captain Murray, "something bad?" He looked wild-eyed at Papa.

Papa had eased, he seemed almost relaxed and funny, sort of elated, which I certainly was not.

"Peritonitis, bad?" he said. "It can spoil your life, if it hits you just right, that's how bad. But we don't have to deal with it here. Your wife has a good chance, I tell you, Murray, if I did my job right."

While they were in the bedroom getting her fixed up I filled the kettle and got out fixings for tea, then I went outdoors. Nobody can possibly appreciate the fresh cool air of just before dawn, or get enough of it with great gulps, unless they've been doing surgery, I thought.

We drank our tea in silence. Papa looked awful, tired, dead beat, but he liked his tea, he said, and looked over at me for quite a long look and smiled. Finally he spoke.

"Can you drive Jet home? It's almost dawn. I'll make a list for you to take to Mama of things I need. I can't leave here."

"Of course," I said. I felt all right again now. He scribbled a list and handed it to me. It was folded over, meaning, of course, I was not to read it.

We went outside. Silas, slumped on the seat of his box wagon, was asleep, his horse too, its old underlip hanging down. Papa petted the old horse, turned him around and gave him a little clip with the whip that made him bolt for home. We both laughed, seeing Silas tumble off the seat onto the floor of the wagon, his legs flaying the air.

Then Jet and I started for home too. It was that gray chill before dawn and it smelled so fresh and good. Of course I pulled Jet to a halt, well out of sight, to read the note. Unfolding it I saw the list of medicines, food, and change of clothing Mama was to get together for James to drive out.

Then I read: "We got the appendix out without its bursting, thank God. Mary Murray has a chance if I did my job right. I think it was a clean job, though a bungling one. Murray was useless, leaving me to choose between Silas (blast him) who followed us, or — a *baby*. Silas was untried and I was not at my best as to jitters anyway. Also his calling didn't add to my ailing self-confidence! So I chose her. She came through (with difficulty) so I'm afraid she's graduated and you and I have lost a baby. I'll get home when I can. H."

The connotation of Silas and a lost "baby" brought before my eyes funerals of babies in little white coffins — babies that didn't make it — and I was intensely displeased, thinking my father might have done better for me than to class me with them.

That's what you get for reading notes you're not supposed to, I said to myself, slapping Jet and driving on. I delivered the note, then delivered myself to the hammock, where I slept all day, determined *never, never* to become a doctor.

12

Without Kody the Prince
Family Could Not Function

PAPA WENT to Medford for commencement; he was only gone a few days. He and Uncle Mort got more alphabet after their names and dressed up like monkeys in red and green hoods and hats with tassels hanging in their eyes.

"And they don't even know enough to call it the *finish* instead of the commencement," said Malcolm disdainfully, resorting to his schoolboy gem — "Jeepers!"

Of course this event diverted Uncle Mort from his intended purpose of moving his family from Nahant to Nantucket to the newly rented house near us. He thought of it when he was once again settled in our house on the island and my father, chuckling with some barely contained joke, called him on the mat. I was present. It was on a Friday. Place: Papa's office.

"Mort," said Papa, his eyes twinkling. "Have you planned how you're going to move Fanny, the children, the maids, and so forth from Nahant down here to the newly rented house?"

Uncle Mort looked troubled.

"How do you mean, *planned*, Harold?"

"Well, train connections, tickets, little things like that. Fanny, being an invalid, can't stand too much stress and strain, you know."

"No, of course she can't." Mustache chewing, furiously, followed.

"Also, have you ordered your horses and carriages from Kenney & Clark? We agreed you should rent, not buy," went on Papa.

"So we did. No, I haven't." Uncle Mort now had a deep crease between his eyes, while Papa's increased in twinkle. He got up and touched a bell and Mary came.

"Ask Kody to come in now, will you, Mary?"

"Yes, Doctor," said Mary, grinning while Uncle Mort in a brown study was observing nothing.

In came a man — I supposed it was anyway. A perfectly stolid-faced person, jaundiced, waxen, his head seemed to tend to a point and was bald except for a thick tuft of hair, giving him the appearance of a tufted grouse.

"Mort," said Papa, rousing the latter, "this is Kody. Kody, this is Dr. Prince."

Kody held out his hand, evidently a clammy one, for Uncle Mort dropped it quickly with an "Ugh!" and then wiped his own on his trouser leg and said sharply, "Never do that again, Kody."

"Yes, sir," said Kody impassively. "I mean no, sir."

Without Kody the Prince Family Could Not Function

Papa laughed and said, "Sit down, Kody, and run over the arrangements for Dr. Prince."

"You mean the move, sir, for Tuesday?"

My father nodded. Kody sat down and began.

"Bridget will have the Beacon Street house comfortable for Mrs. Prince to spend the night after coming up from Nahant. I have cabs engaged the next day to get them all to the South Station for the train trip to Woods Hole, and staterooms spoken for on the ferry. Kenney & Clark will have the horses there and I selected a victoria for Mrs. Prince and a basket phaeton; also, Dr. Williams, though you didn't mention it, I thought two ponies would go good, one for Miss Clare, the other for Master Morton — you did give me free rein, Doctor?" The yellow face turned anxiously towards Papa.

"Quite right, Kody. You are opening the house here to have it comfortable for Mrs. Prince?"

"Yes, sir, and I would like Dr. Prince to come over with me to select the room he thinks she would prefer before I make up the beds. I've a sort of makeshift lunch prepared for him, sir, if he will come now with me."

Uncle Mort looked curiously now at Kody. "Haven't I seen you somewhere before, Kody?"

"Yes, sir, most every day last winter, sir. I was janitor at the Medical School, till Dr. Williams engaged me to be your nur — . . . valet, sir."

"Right the first time, Kody," said Papa.

I was surprised how Uncle Mort took all these plans for granted until I realized how Papa had nursed him through college and Aunt Fanny (poor soul) took over from her sickroom to look after him after that.

69

"When did you say my family are coming, Kody?" asked Uncle Mort.

"Tuesday, sir," impassively.

"And what's today?"

"Friday, sir."

"Well then," said Uncle Mort, getting up. "We'd better get going and select that room, the sunniest one, with a view of the ocean, for Mrs. Prince. By the way, is there a stable with the house for the brats' ponies? I didn't notice."

"Yes, sir," said Kody.

"Come along then. What have you for my lunch? I think I'm hungry, Kody."

Together they left. Papa called in Mama and Mary too, and putting his head back, burst out laughing.

"A perfect fit. I never did a better job in my life. I was nervous for a minute, they got off to a bad start, but Kody is able to commandeer anything."

Papa went to the window, followed by Mama and Mary.

"There they go," went on Papa. "There goes the most brilliant mind I know or have ever known, and without the common sense of the average donkey. And a poker-faced, practical, competent automaton. And you know, Mama, Mort not only showed no surprise but I'll be bound he thinks it's always been just the way it is now, with Kody all settled in."

"Will Kody mesh with Mort's peculiarities, do you think?" asked Mama. "For he has plenty, bless his heart."

"Kody admires him profoundly, spent half the winter reading Mort's book, or trying to," said Papa.

"Oh, Mrs. Williams, I never read Dr. Prince's book," said Mary, "nor could I, but he's one of the lovingest gentlemen, so kind and always sorry to bother a body. We all love him."

"We certainly do, Mary; all of us love him. I didn't mean to criticize him, only his sometimes strange ways," replied Mama. "Like his thinking his family would get down here by remote control. He's devoted to Mrs. Prince. I can't say as much for the children, alas, but he misses her woefully even though it took Dr. Williams to get her here."

We were delighted to have Aunt Fanna move next door — too bad she moved the "saps" too, but I suppose it is customary to bring one's own children.

I loved her. I called her Aunt Fanna instead of Fanny because a temporary vacancy in my tooth department made it easier that way and the name stuck, even after the new tooth arrived. Malcolm said the only reason I loved her was because I ate my first sweet potato at her house but that wasn't true — there were other important reasons too.

Aunt Fanna had a long face and a longish nose and sat in a rocking chair most of the time — there had been an accident of some kind which was never spoken of. She also had an insane sister who, I believe, drowned herself at Nantucket. I'm not sure about this as I was very young and so put to bed while all the excitement of it was discussed downstairs, which was really too bad. However, as Malcolm said (occasionally he had an idea), this way we didn't have to be bothered with an extra aunt, so it was just as well she did drown.

Before her accident Aunt Fanna gave birth to Uncle Mort's two children, which also was too bad, because after the accident maybe she couldn't have had them, and they

were definitely "saps." Clare, the eldest, was eight and I
was four when I ate my sweet potato, and she was very
toplofty about it and remarked in my hearing that "nobody
who knew anything of the world would coo and crow so
over a sweet potato!" She had very large brown eyes, which
would have looked nice in anyone else, and when Mama
picked me up after lunch she said to Aunt Fanna, "Fanny,
Clare has your eyes," which wasn't true, for Clare still had
her own when I looked.

Morton, as he was always called, was the exact image of
Uncle Mort on the outside, but that was all. They looked
awfully funny walking together (which they rarely did, not
liking each other much), and Aunt Fanna from her rocking
chair got quivery when they did go for a walk because
Uncle Mort, forgetting Morton was beside him, often
walked off in a different direction and left him alone on
the sidewalk. Uncle Mort walked very fast anyway and
when an idea pricked him he almost galloped. Morton
was afraid of crabs, horses too, and especially of being left
on the sidewalk alone — he really was quite distasteful to
us. We never sought the company of either Morton or
Clare.

Another thing — they had clean fingernails and a gover-
ness who told me I smelt intolerably of the barn and that
Malcolm had the "horrors of Hell" in his pockets. The
whole batch of them were really a poor lot, we felt. I asked
Uncle Mort if we had to see them much when they came
to Nantucket and he just laughed and said, "I know what
you mean — rough them up, little Alice, when you do
meet."

One day when I was climbing up the side of Uncle Mort's

barn, Michael tickled my legs with a whip because he said I was getting dust to fall on his harnesses. I fell spread-eagled on a carriage jack and hurt myself awfully. Papa said I must lie on a bed for two or three days, so as he was having lumbago on his bed and I didn't want the boringness of being alone on a bed, I asked Aunt Fanna if I could lie on hers and she said, "Of course, I wish you belonged to me anyway."

[13]

The Wild Ponies from Minnesota

THE OLD SIDE-WHEELER tied up at the dock one sunny June noonday. The passengers disembarked, wondering why the gangplank was pulled up before the freight came off and why the wharf was so crowded with spectators. Spectators tense with excitement and apprehension — like that feeling in the dentist's waiting-room before the tooth is pulled. From their attitudes, danger must be in that imprisoned hold. Someone's foot on a bicycle pedal, the other one on the ground implied instant flight, another's hands gripped the low freight house roof for a sudden vault atop it. Papa standing close to the ferry, a revolver in his back pocket. What did all this mean?

A wide pathway had been cleared from ferry to paddock — our paddock. It was lined solid with boys and men, each one holding something defensively, a fish-hook shovel, broom, rake, anything with a long handle apparently to ward off whatever was going to charge out of the hold. Malcolm and I, idling sideways on our ponies and chewing gum vigorously, looked with contempt across the pathway at a fat off-island boy on a very old pinto, knock-kneed and dozing. This boy stood high in his stirrups, twirling a lasso and quivering with excitement from his spurs to his five-gallon hat.

Suddenly the Captain called out from the pilot house window, "Shove the gangplank across now, boys, and put them high sides onto her. Be sure you cinch 'em good on top with those there ropes." Lowering his voice, he said to Papa, "I counted thirty, Doc. They all got tags tied to their manes sayin' they come from Minnesoty — awful scairt and nervous-like, but real pretty, like a bug's ear."

A rumor ran about the spectators. "So it's true. Dr. Williams really has imported a carload of wild ponies from the West for his children to break this summer. How does he dare take such a risk?"

"I'll tell you how," said an old fisherman crossly, who incidentally availed himself of the opportunity to stand behind a huge wooden pile the ferry's hawser latched onto. "It's 'cause he knows his kids can ride and I *mean* ride. Ain't no grasshopper born quick as little Alice, she be all over a pony 'fore he gets done a-lookin' at her. Malcolm same thing. She being so small, it's more eye-catchin', is the only difference. Doc knows what he's doin'."

"Be you ready, boys?" yelled the Captain.

"Aye, aye, sir," from the dock hands.

"Let 'er rip, Andy!" and the bars in the ferry's hold were pulled aside.

A rush of wind, a clatter of hooves as thirty terrified

ponies jammed the gangplank and headed on full gallop down the pathway cleared for them, amidst shouts and roars from the men waving their implements to keep them within its bounds. The fat boy, seeing the oncoming stampede head straight at him, panicked, got snarled up in his lasso, lost his balance, and plunged into the ocean, while the pinto, old as he was, pricked up his ears and joined in the race. So did a few carriage horses, who tried to kick loose from the shafts, snort back their youth with raised eager heads, and join in the mad rush of their kin as best they could.

A shout, "Pony overboard!" — a crashing sound, followed in a couple of minutes by a shot.

Malcolm and I had ridden ahead to join Clint Folger, James Fox, and Michael. We all stood abreast across the street, waving whips and shouting so as to turn the onrushing ponies into our paddock and close the gate on them.

The crowd of spectators hurried up the now safe pathway to get a closer look, and every kid stood awed, dazed, and silent, gazing at the milling ponies. Malcolm and I slid off our mounts, put a rein through an arm, and spit — a long, slow, impressive *spit*. This was our day — even if not real cowboys, we could spit like them. The kids outside our barnyard looked impressed, mightily so.

After everyone had gone home and the street was clear, Papa was seen walking slowly towards us, his head bowed. Clint went right up to him.

"Did she break her leg, Doctor?" he asked solicitously.

"I'm not sure, but I think she must have. Anyway, tangled in between the ferry and the wharf piles, struggling there in the water and so terrified — I thought what with the terrible difficulty of getting her out, she'd had enough."

"Terrible money loss, Doctor," said James Fox gloomily. "Likely best *polo* pony o' the lot." Papa glared. James saw me come over and take Papa's hand, and came to his senses. Cheerfully he piped up, "Ain't them a pretty lot, Doctor? All colors — blacks, chisnuts, sauls, dabbled grays, and Holy Mother of God, will you look at the manure caked on them whites!"

"I'm not blind, James," said Papa crossly. "I see them all."

I squeezed his hand. He smiled down at me. "Have you picked out the first one you want to break yet?" he asked.

"Yep, that black mare standing by the hayrack, with a blaze and three white feet."

"She's a beauty," said Papa. "And you, Malcolm?"

"The strawberry roan there — looks too mean for Alice, with that Roman nose. He's bigger too than the others." I glared at him.

"Well," said Papa to Clint Folger. "Let's all of us men separate those two and put one each in the two corrals on the other side of the barn away from the other ponies for the night."

"First," said Clint, "to make easier catching and roping, how about James and me getting up in the hayloft and throwing down some of that nice green timothy you were so smart to raise? Smart too, Doctor, to build the hayrack the whole length of the barn for plenty space to feed."

Papa looked cheered a little and I went over and hugged Clint. Then Malcolm and I left and went to the house to make our preparations for the next morning. Boots had to be oil-soaked, belt too, for on my belt I hung the short rope I used; then to the cellar for big winter carrots, their faded foliage still on, so that filling my back pockets they looked like a plumed tail floating behind me.

I sat next morning on the fence of the corral. Green New England eyes looked on black Western ones, a query in each pair. The black mare couldn't move about much, the corral was too restricted — her hayrack and water tub were fastened outside it. She was quieter, tired, rough-coated, and watchful. She eyed me suspiciously, then turned her back, until the strong pungent smell of the carrot I began to eat turned her back to investigate.

Bite after bite I took, she watched, stamped one foot. I held out the carrot. She snatched it from me, and while she was munching it, I slipped my rope into her mouth and over her head and slid down into the corral. With a snort, she dropped the carrot and struck at me with her front feet, but I was on her back by that time.

She shivered all over and looked around as if to say, "How in the world did this grasshopper in boots get on top of me?"

With one foot, while Papa watched, laughing, I kicked open the corral gate and we were off. She started on the wrong lead, which annoyed her and, in shifting, she nearly threw me with a sudden stop and jerk, anchored as I was only by her mane and the taut short rope in her mouth passed over her ears and held in my hand. Smart, she sensed this, stopped, pawed, and threw her head up and down fast — it didn't work. I still had the rope, so then she reared and I slid way forward on her neck and sawed on her mouth till the delicate lips bled; she was too near falling backwards for both our comfort.

Snorting, she broke into a run, round and round the field,

78

a wild gallop that I loved. At last she slowed, panting, to a stop. I pulled out one of my tail feathers, bit into it, and leaning forward offered her the rest of it as I slid off her back. After a moment's look at me she took the carrot, but her mouth hurt and she frothed.

I felt it would be safe enough to ease her bleeding lips by taking the rope out of her mouth and passing it round her neck, but I was wrong. She was off in a bound, but I was on her back. After some more foolishness she stopped by her discarded carrot and finished it and, tired out, let me lead her back to the corral, disheartened. Her first lesson was over, she accepted me as a queer though carrot-eating kind of creature, and it's always been in my experience the *first* lesson that sets the curriculum.

I named her Shimmo, a lovely Indian name for a point on the island. I had her four years, broke her to harness, and also jumped her. She won two reds and one yellow at the Riding Club in Boston in combination and as a jumper.

Malcolm's roan proved a devil, loved to bite and kick and was reluctant to do otherwise, had never joined the carrot union, and had a mean eye. But Malcolm's little steel Cossack whip, which he wore in his boot, wrapped around the pony's rump repeatedly and left my brother finally the victor, and to ease the humiliation to the roan we named *him* Victor.

This method was repeated. Papa caught the ponies to be put in the corral, feeling that while we could cope with one at a time, a charging-about mob was too much. As each pony got his or her degree (we were co-educational) it was put back with the unbroken ones to share its knowledge.

The old pinto helped too; he came to live with us after

the wreckage of spurs and five-gallon hat. The other ponies loved him, and nose to nose on hot summer days they swapped yarns of their youth on the prairies. We called him Merrylegs, after Black Beauty's friend.

After they were all "broke," time hung heavy, and so did my wrist in its plaster cast. But once I was out of that cast, we took up circus riding, eventually getting quite proficient in standing up, a foot on each back of two ponies tied side by side and galloping round the field, and at summer's end adding a third pony tandem. We were both insufferable in our showing off to the many bystanders who loitered along the street.

At the end of the summer we had a few fast-gaited ponies, good for polo. Letters went out from Papa, buyers arrived, and fancy prices for the good ones, moderate purchases of the rest for riding schools left Papa with a profit and us with a glorious summer's sport. And me, the owner of my Shimmo!

[14]

William Gillette

BECAUSE no Hamlet ever came near Booth's in greatness nor a Cordelia anywhere near Ellen Terry's, my father refused to go and see lesser luminaries and took his Shakespeare between the covers.

'Sconset, a small community, consisted of a very tiny winter population, but in the summer it blossomed into a brilliant group of off-island actors, Ellen Terry, William Gillette, and many others equally well known.

Although it was only seven miles from Nantucket center, getting to 'Sconset on a first visit to the island on a foggy night was like crossing the Himalayas. The ferry landing of course at Nantucket, the trip to 'Sconset was made by horse and wagon, and as neither horse nor actor knew where they were headed except by the name 'Sconset, matters became complicated. The horse, superior navigator of the two, could find his way home to Nantucket even though the fog was so thick he could barely see his own whiskers; but the word 'Sconset was not included in his education and he was dependent in getting there upon the stupidity of man or, in this case, actor.

Once they were set upon the road by some scornful native who didn't want them there anyway and considered all actors mental hazards, the road was straight enough. All that was required was getting out of the wagon at intervals and on hands and knees feeling for the edges, to be sure one was on the road — rather wet and soggy compared to the Broadway they had left, and sure to induce nostalgia.

I was four, maybe three, when Ellen Terry, still ambulatory, joined the actors' group at 'Sconset for the summer. She was said to be still beautiful — a "rose petal in a pot-pourri jar" type of exquisiteness — and her voice had lost none of its magic. So when she condescended to give a playlet called *Little Sally in the Buttercups* in our Sea Cliff Inn theater it was deemed essential by my parents that I should be exposed to this great actress.

Every ticket was taken and magic lanterns hung at the entrance of the Sea Cliff surrounding a banner in her honor fluttering in the breeze: "Ellen Terry — all Nantucket appreciates the honor of your presence here."

Awakened in the depths of night — every accursed hair pulled around a curling stick, hopefully to hold its curl for an hour or two in a wet fog — boiled, starched, and completely furious — I was seated between my parents in the front row of the little theater.

"Little Sally is going to pick the pretty buttercups, baby," whispered Mama soothingly, "Won't that be nice?"

"Damn the nassy buttercups," said I quite audibly,

straight from the James Fox vocabulary, so Mama, after a shattered look around, sighed and desisted.

An announcer came before the curtain and a hush followed as he said, "We are most sorry that Miss Terry feels unable to risk the long drive in the fog, and we are obliged to cancel her performance tonight. However, Mr. William Gillette has most kindly offered to give us *Dr. Jekyll and Mr. Hyde*, a role for which he is renowned."

My parents exchanged agonized looks. There they sat in the front row of a little theater filled to capacity, a young, infuriated buffalo between them, quite capable of charging. Should they try it or was the better part of valor to take the animal home? Desperately they wanted to see Gillette.

"Let's try it," said Papa. "She's so tired out with rage she may doze off. Anyway she couldn't possibly take it in."

"All right," said Mama and they settled back comfortably in their seats.

The curtain went up — the scene a drawing room with a piano in it. (Will I ever forget it!) Dr. Jekyll, bland, fat, smiling, was talking to a young lady, and in an audible voice I remarked, "He very nice old man," but before I could be properly admonished the stage darkened and creeping around the piano came Mr. Hyde.

With a loud shriek of undisguised terror the young buffalo held forth — shriek followed shriek. The curtain had to be lowered, no Mr. Gillette could possibly be heard above the din. A discomfited Papa carried me out, followed by an embarrassed Mama. What happened to the play I never knew. I suppose it followed tradition: the play must go on.

Years later, at the age of thirty or so, I found myself one

day in a launch on the Connecticut River at Lyme and above it on the hills the so-called Gillette Castle. A wild idea entered my head.

"Stop at the pier of Mr. Gillette's castle," I told our boatman. "I want to see him."

"Rats," said the pilot. "Mr. Gillette sees no one. He's very old and lives secluded with only Japanese servants. You couldn't possibly see him."

"Nevertheless I'll try," I said firmly, and he tied up at the little dock. I walked up to a huge iron gate, over which a bell hung. Deep-throated dogs barked in the fenced enclosure as I pulled the bell. A Japanese man came running lightly down a path; he was dressed in a white coat, evidently a butler.

"I want to see Mr. Gillette," I said to him.

He shook his head violently.

"Mr. Gillette see nobody," he said emphatically.

"I think he may see me," I said and, opening my purse, I gave the man a five-dollar bill and a card on which I wrote, "Do you remember a 'brat' that stopped your Mr. Hyde at the Sea Cliff Inn, Nantucket, some twenty-six or twenty-seven years ago? I'm that brat and want to apologize, now I'm old enough to talk and not just scream."

He took the note and the money and, still shaking his head, disappeared up the path. He was gone a long time; I almost despaired. One good sign, however — the dogs stopped barking. Perhaps they were being tied up. Then the man in the white coat appeared. He unlocked the gate and said rather disagreeably, "Follow me, please."

Up a long winding path we climbed, the "castle" looming high above us, its turrets and battlements silhouetted against

84

the sky. Rounding a sharp curve, I saw a very old gentleman with silvery hair standing smiling. As I got closer to
him he held out both hands and said in the voice of
Dr. Jekyll, "My dear young lady, no, no, no apologies. I
took it as one of the greatest tributes of my long career!"

We had a lovely time, sitting on his terrace and chatting
over cookies and lemonade. He was very old and stooped
but his magnetism and charm were young as ever!

[15]

An Hour with Grover Cleveland

PRESIDENT CLEVELAND CAME on a visit to Nantucket when I was eight years old and I spent an hour all alone with him — a memorable and privileged occasion. He was a very warm, lovable person and always, when I saw him, laughing.

That summer my brother Malcolm and a vacationing professor had put together a small steam engine. From magazine ads on the mainland a tiny hod car and one diminutive passenger car had been obtained. The track, which local help volunteered in laying, ran from the boat wharf in Nantucket through the outskirts of the village proper, then by the fair grounds, along the moors past Tom Nevers Head to 'Sconset, a total of seven miles.

Enthusiasm high, scientific efficiency was at a very low point! The trial run took an hour and a half, together with a display on the part of the two engineers of extreme cau-

86

tion and apprehension. The little engine gave peculiar snorts and squeals indicative of one of many possible disasters in construction, but the goal — taking the famous visitor about to visit the island — necessitated haste, so prayers replaced probing into these strange noises. The track was laid on ties, which were themselves in many sections on clear sand, wobbly to an uncomfortable degree. The pace was slower than that of Shimmo, whom I had to hold back as we rode alongside.

Then, on a lovely, warm August day, President Cleveland boarded the little passenger car with my cousin Henry Bigelow Williams to make the trip to 'Sconset. All of the island folk turned out to see them off. As the President waved, trying to include everyone, with his great expanse of billowing white shirt and his large, smiling, kindly, ruddy face, no one could have been more at one with them all. Up front, in snowy white coveralls and long visored caps on which Mama had embroidered in somewhat dizzy red letters "Nantucket, 'Sconset R.R. Co.," Malcolm and the professor were solemn and important as they oiled — doubtless praying all the while — every available joint and nut.

Off it started, that hateful little monster, puffing and snorting sententiously as it inched its way through the town. The whistle blast at a crossing was a bit of unnecessary showing off; every islander who couldn't see or hear it knew what was happening. Then something stuck; it couldn't stop whistling. The piercing sound penetrated the very marrow of one's bones. Ten full minutes it shrieked before the "engineers" could silence it. People went about with their mouths open to relieve the pressure on their aching eardrums.

We finally made it over the crossing and onto the moors. I, on Shimmo, rode slowly alongside. Laying the track in sand had presented scientific problems that apparently were not solved: one section now loosened and jumped up before the little engine, slapping it rudely in the nose.

Cousin Henry, an old man of forty-five, was also a president — president of the Nantucket, 'Sconset R.R. Co. He seemed to be taking everything far more seriously than his fellow Chief Executive, who was enjoying the incident and vibrating with laughter. Until then, I had thought the job of President of the United States was the more worrisome one.

I had always secretly admired my mother's gracious, hospitable manner, and since she wasn't around, I decided to try my hand at copying it. Spanking clean (for once) in white riding breeches and boots, I stepped forward, curtsied, and extended my hand to the enormous President, asking, "May I help you down and take you over that little hill to a beautiful patch of wild flowers I know are there, while they fix up the track?"

He smiled broadly and put one large finger in my hand as he climbed down, smiling more and more. "I should like that very much," he said. "But what about your pony?"

"Oh, Shimmo will stand still when her rein is down. She was taught that," I told him.

Finger in hand, we strolled over the soft turf, up the little hill, and stood looking down on the magical carpet of color — wild sweet peas, bluets, rosa rugosa. Bees buzzed, in the far distance the breakers boomed, overhead white clouds sailed in the blue sky. There was no habitation, nothing but undulating moors to the horizon, and silence. President Cleveland heaved a deep sigh and stretched out contentedly on the soft turf. But I, feeling my mother would do still more, had an idea. Fumbling in my pocket (I always traveled with a larder), I drew out some battered-looking animal crackers, mixed with some lint and I hate to think what else. I looked at him, lying there so big and long. His eyes were closed.

"President Cleveland," I ventured, "would you like some animal crackers? I've found some in my pocket."

Instantly he sat upright and smiled. "I'd love some," he said. "I haven't had any for thirty or forty years. I'd love to have some once again."

I handed them to him. Some — not many — were whole. Mostly they were tails and ears, but he seemed to enjoy them. "Are you hungry?" he asked. "Always," I replied. "Me too," he said, and we both laughed. How I liked him!

When he finished eating, he sighed again. "This is a very beautiful place you've brought me to. One feels God is very close."

"Yes," I answered. "President Cleveland, will you be all right with God a little while if I go and see how they're getting on with the track?"

Tears accompanied his booming laughter. "I hope I will," he said, wiping his eyes. "You go right along."

I ran back. The other president was asleep in the car. It seemed to tire them being presidents. My brother and the professor were all dirty and cross as bears, but nearly finished. Shimmo was all right too, nibbling at the grass and stamping flies. I guess Malcolm was jealous that I'd had

President Cleveland all to myself while the president in the car had slept all the time, so he ran ahead of me and blurted out.

"We're ready now, your . . . highness. The track is all laid." President Cleveland then really roared with laughter and my brother felt so foolish. I was glad of that. "All right, my boy," he put one hand on my brother's shoulder, the other on my head, and we sauntered back.

Cousin Henry awakened, got out of the car and made a great fuss getting the other President in and seated again. The rest of the trip was uneventful.

My mother and father, who were coming to bring the President home, had driven the seven miles over to 'Sconset in our yellow horse-drawn wagon. President Cleveland shook hands with them, still laughing, and apologized to my mother for being without a coat.

Then he looked over at me. "Are you hungry?" I nodded. "Me too," he said. "I want all of you to come to the Tea House as my guests. And this young lady," he put his hand on my head, "I shall make a Roving Ambassadress. She's cut out for the diplomatic service." He told them about my taking him to the wild flowers and all the rest. My parents laughed but I was worried, not having come to any of those long words in *Stepping Stones to Literature*.

The tea was gorgeous and I gorged! The "engineers" were pretty dirty, but happy, especially when President Cleveland wrote on a card of his how he'd enjoyed the trip and told them they could pin it up in the cab of the nasty little engine. I call it nasty — he didn't.

16

Surfside as It Was Then

THE DIVERSITY of the sea's activities around our island is one of its charms. Roaring surf at Surfside and Madaket necessitated in those early days life-saving stations at each of those sites; along the harbor and the jetty too, smooth placid waters were conducive to boating and swimming. I learned to swim in the harbor, after swallowing half of it; Papa would walk in front of me, his hand under my chin, then take his hand away suddenly and let me sink.

But we learned never to trust the sea, even in its quiet moments. The harbor came into our cellar in the Line Storm; even those quiet waters didn't always behave themselves. The sea took back land as well as gave it when a furious storm was unleashed.

Another surprising thing about the sea was its shoals. Old fishermen who knew the sea like the palm of their hand — fishermen who needed no weather bureau, for they

91

could dip a finger in the sea, hold it up to the wind, and prognosticate to a certainty what was ahead — they told us and I believe them that one could walk on the shoals from Nantucket to Chappaquiddick on Martha's Vineyard and never get in deeper than two and one-half feet of water.

But Surfside — a magnificent stretch of the Atlantic, reaching uninterrupted from Nantucket Island to the shores of Spain — was unique. Huge combers rolled up in their curling power, broke and pounded upon the beach in thunderous roars, then sucked their way back into the sea over the shifting sands they had inundated with spray, in a tricky undertow. No man ventured into this surf unless securely roped and then but very seldom. For death lurked in this magnificence of ocean. Above the beach on the high sandy bluffs was also desolation — a life-saving station, a slowly disintegrating summer hotel, the only habitations.

In semidarkness one night, several hours before dawn, a lone man slid down the cliff to the beach. He stripped and, flinging his shirt and trousers onto the sand, he plunged into the breakers. It was my father. Worn by a night's vigil by the bedside of a typhoid patient, sickened by the torpor and smells of the sickroom, he longed for the refreshment of the sea. After some time, revived and rejuvenated, he decided to come ashore, but found he could not. The undertow repeatedly pulled him back into the sea; on the sliding, shifting sand was no purchase to be had.

At first he laughed aloud. "What, with *my* strength . . ." — but he could not hear his own laugh over the roar of the breakers. Then he cursed — and could not hear his curses either. Apprehensive then, he tried again and again, using more and more strength to gain the beach. It was futile. The undertow sucked him back each time.

Fear struck. He was sweating and cold at the same time; his heart began to pound. He glimpsed his shirt and trousers flung so carelessly on the beach — so flat and empty they looked — and he shuddered. Was it possible that one mistake, one foolhardy, arbitrary mistake could cut off life? He thought of my mother, of us, of his ardor for living. He tried to fight the realization that it was possible, very possible, that only those discarded clothes on the beach would be traceable. He was getting winded and exhausted.

"I must think," he groaned, and swam out beyond the breakers to float on his back in the quieter waters. As if to a rhythmic cradle's rocking, he gave himself to the soothing motion of the waves and fought for control while he rested in it. But fear would not leave him and it pricked his mind with tormenting thoughts. Perhaps, he shuddered, cruising sharks might lurk in these quieter waters, for a whale had foundered here once and both were deep water inmates.

As his heart slowed and his breathing eased, a vestige of a plan crossed his mind. He would try it. With a gleam of hope in his heart, he rode the breakers, then on hands and knees he dug into the retreating sand under him with toes and fingernails in a frenzy of strength. Twice he failed. The third time he gained dry sand and lay gasping on the beach too exhausted to rise. But not his mind — that was active as he went on thinking.

"How dare a man be arbitrary in the face of such an adversary? Probably he deserves to drown and certainly he must learn humility if he does not."

He was pretty well shaken when he joined us at breakfast and told us the whole story, ending with "Never lived a man happier or more grateful to climb into a pair of trousers and a shirt." Uncle Mort came over and had to hear it again; his eyes like Mama's were misty. Kody, James Fox, and the "girls" who were all standing listening in the pantry whispered in chorus, "Thank God!"

17

Just Bud

Two LIGHTSHIPS, *Cross Rip* and *Tuckernuck Shoals*, were firmly anchored in the tricky waters between Woods Hole and Nantucket, and with the incessant ringing of their bells warned off all approaching ships. These two ships gleamed and glistened in a dazzling purity of white paint and could be seen for miles in the sunshine. Never a spot of dirt appeared anywhere on the halyards or hull but one of the nine government-appointed men who manned the ships climbed up to obliterate it with his paint pail and brush.

Keeping their ship a glistening white may have somehow eased the realization of their own contrasting blackened characters, for these men were drawn from the dregs of humanity to serve a three-month stretch of complete isolation from the outside world. In long periods of fog the bells clanged day and night, otherwise lights supplanted them during nighttime. The men passed the time in fishing, painting, or playing cards in relaxed moments, an occasional murder in the less relaxed ones. Sometimes a maverick signed up, seeing Paradise in being incommunicado from a vitriolic wife and still being able to put long-distance bread on the table from his small paycheck.

Papa was examining the men for physical defects which would forbid their assignment to duty. This took place at the Nantucket Athletic Club. Malcolm and I begged to go as Mama, loaded with sweaters and socks she had knit, was going with him to give them to the men, and we were given permission to go too. All charitable thoughts left her soul, however, as she saw her two offspring rush at one large, lethal-looking customer, unshaven and fierce, and clasp him adoringly round the knees while screaming, "Lefty!" Papa's stethoscope played a polka dance, I guess, for he lowered it quickly to give Mama first aid.

It was our Boston garbage man (called "swill" man in those days) with whom Malcolm and I had had many a delightful chat over the backyard fence. He was getting off the garbage truck in favor of his wife's brother and taking a sabbatical of three months from "wifey."

Mama was really shattered and said later to Papa, "I suppose you condone it. All I can see is the other side of the aisle as you lead little Alice to the altar, the swill men and wives of greater Boston lining the pews. Why, oh why must I endure these moments?"

Another year when Malcolm and I attended the line-up, we watched Papa standing on tiptoe to take heart soundings on a huge man, also unshaven, fiercer-looking than a grizzly, while beside him stood a slender boy.

"Looks like a good-for-nothing girl," whispered my

brother. "Look at those dreamy eyes and long eyelashes — not a sign of a respectable whisker on him."

The stethoscope lingered a long time on this boy's sunken chest; at last Papa spoke, after a long, piercing look at him. "You seem weak, run down, lad, do you feel ill?"

The large blue eyes were raised to his, but before he could answer, the grizzly bear next to him slung an arm over the boy's shoulder and spoke.

"Bud here ain't eat, Doc. I found him on the waterfront, going in he were. Please, Doc, pass him. I'll see he gets filled up."

The boy had a little roll, smaller than the other men's rolls. Papa touched it.

"What's in there, Bud, and what's your other name? There's only a blank here on my list."

"My paints, sir, and I ain't got no other name, just Bud."

"He paints pitchers, Doc," said the grizzly quickly. "He'll give you one, they're real pretty pitchers."

"All right," said Papa after a pause. "I'll pass him, but I'll be out earlier than my usual inspection to have another look at him."

The boy was trembling under the great protective arm of the grizzly as they moved away towards the little government boat, the *Petrel*, that was to carry them to the lightship. This little steel boat was used to catch swordfish (thought to be inedible in those days) and a one-dollar bounty was paid to catch and kill one and tow him out to sea to dump — for they eat the good fish.

Papa said sadly as we left the Athletic Club, "That pitiful boy Bud is like a sword through my heart. He's a potential tubercular victim, I'm afraid, unless Ben can mother him. How extraordinary a friendship — a potential killer and a supersensitive, ailing lad."

The summer wore on, as summers do, keeping its future events hidden. We had the longest spell of fog I ever remember; the lightship was swathed in it as in a shroud. The daily newspaper barely reached its target from the ferry, guided only by the bells which rang incessantly day and night as the ship rocked to the sea's motion. To and fro — ding, dong, ding, dong — the bells rang from a phantom ship, at once there and not there, and the foggy weather continued sultry, wet, dripping.

One night as we were eating supper, all the windows wide open, we heard the booming voice of Captain Barker of the *Island Home,* and his large red face peered into our candlelit dining room.

"Trouble, Doc, on the *Cross Rip.* Their megaphone come through the fog and I shut my engines off to be sure to get it good. 'Send Doc out — we got a lunatic on board' come over the waves. ' 'E's cornered in the bow bottom deck screamin' and wavin' a knife. Send Doc pronto.' "

Then he added, "The *Petrel* is cleanin' 'erself up after swordin' and will be ready come dawn. All right, Doc?"

"All right," said Papa meditatively.

"Can we go too?" I asked.

"I guess so." Papa's voice was sad.

"Well really, Papa!" Mama flashed her eyes, but he neither saw nor heard, only said, "I wish Mort was on the island — this is his line."

It was not yet light as the little *Petrel* bounded over the waves around Brant Point and out to sea.

Just Bud

"Git in the cabin, little Alice, and fix us bacon and eggs. Coffee's already a'bilin'," said Captain Barrett. "Smells a mite too bloody in there fer Malcolm's stomick."

"Jeepers, I wish I could trade," whispered Malcolm to me. "Your stomach is a waste on a girl."

Papa meanwhile sat in the bow, his medicine bag beside him, a canvas thing with straps on it on his knees. He looked terribly troubled, so when I handed him his tray of bacon and eggs I took his other hand. He smiled at me and said gently, "I blame myself, baby. I'm sure it's Bud. I shouldn't have let him go."

The sun was out, the sea was choppy, our little craft snorted and bounded through the whitecaps. Malcolm, sick as a dog, lay moaning on the deck. Captain Barrett chewed like mad and scowled; after a gigantic spit he shouted to Papa.

"You ain't a-goin' to venture in arter that critter, him holdin' a knife, be ye, Doc?"

"It's not that that worries me, Sam, it's my own bad judgment."

We neared the lightship, men were crowded at the rail. The *Petrel* gave her little snorting whistle and the big anchored ship answered.

"I ain't goin' a mite closer," said our captain, picking up his megaphone.

"Put out!" he hollered into it. "I'm afeared o' the wash."

"He's afraid of being knifed," whispered Malcolm, empty now and bouncy as a top.

A skiff was lowered, and a huge man, must be Grizzly, got in and rowed over to us where we hung off with engines idling. It was Grizzly, I saw, as he pulled alongside us. Papa was already slipping over the rail, looking at the ravaged face below.

"It's Bud, Ben?"

The big man nodded — he had difficulty getting out the words. " 'Twas the bells, Doc — druv Bud mad. He kep' a-beggin' me to have 'em stop, kep' a-jumpin' into my arms, then a-kneelin' 'fore 'em and a prayin'."

Papa, holding the canvas bag, which I saw now was a sort of coat with the ends of the arms sewed up, handed his medicine bag to Ben and got in the skiff. Ben rowed them to the lightship.

We bobbed about on the waves and waited. Suddenly the screaming stopped. Then some men lowered a body into the skiff, Ben took the oars, and Papa got in the stern.

Reaching us, Ben and Papa laid Bud on the deck. He was in the straitjacket, which was way too big and hung on him in folds. Captain Barrett seemed ready to take refuge in the skiff, but Papa said, "I've given Bud some morphia, Sam — you needn't fear — he won't awake for hours."

Captain Barrett climbed back again. Together we stood looking down on the prostrate form; the face was sunken and very pale. In contrast, a lock of bright hair lay on the forehead. Ben was crying, unashamed, a great rough giant in tears. Suddenly he put his hand in his jacket and pulled out a painting. He laid it on the deck beside Bud.

"Ain't it realsome, Doc?" he said.

Malcolm and I looked too. It was a picture of the sea, like this sea day, all shimmering in the sun. We looked at both the picture and the real sea; we couldn't tell the difference.

Just Bud

"My God!" said Papa in an awed kind of whisper.

"Bud, he tore up all the others and threw 'em at the bells. I had this one — he done give it to me way back," and Ben ran a huge paw under his nose, as he picked up the picture and put it back in his blouse. Then he turned toward the skiff.

"You'll let me hear 'bout Bud, Doc? How he do in that hospital you're going to take him to?"

He put a leg over the rail and paused.

"Life ain't never goin' to be the same again 'thout Bud, he made me see a whole lot o' things different, takin' care o' him like I was."

"Yes, Ben, I want Dr. Prince to see him when I take him to Boston tomorrow, but I wouldn't count on too much." Papa was almost crying himself.

Two years later, during the "equinoctial," a loud knock sounded on our big front door at Nantucket as we huddled around a peat fire. It was Ben. He looked years older, cleaned up, a nice grizzly now with kind, sad eyes.

"Bud's dead, Doc, died two weeks ago at the Taunton Asylum. I been goin' reglar to check but he never knowed me. I took his pitcher to the Art Museum and them experts 'oh'd' and 'ah'd' somethin' fierce, called it 'pure native genius' — so I left it with 'em and tol' 'em the whole story o' Bud. Warn't it a pity, Doc?" And Ben blew his nose.

"It was," said Papa gently. "Dr. Prince believed it was a brain tumor, inevitably fatal, and that the aggravation of the bells only hastened the end."

After a long pause Papa said, "What are you doing, Ben? Can't we put you up for the night? It's a wicked one."

"Thankee, Doc, I'm bunkin' wi' Captain Barrett. He's

offered me a job swordin' and I might as well take it as do anythin' else, I guess."

We all shook hands, and Papa held the front door with all his strength against the battering wind and rain as Ben went out into the black night.

18

We Move to Boston in the Fall

FOR YEARS I thought Labor Day meant the horrendous labor of packing up after the summer and leaving Nantucket. I thought so until I was sixteen and it was explained to me by Papa as I drank my first "allowed" cup of coffee.

The move to Boston was always dated so many days after Labor Day and was a time of great sadness to Malcolm and me. First, two huge wooden crates that took six men to budge when filled were placed near the piazza for handy packing. They rested on a "jigger," a low flat-bottomed wagon. The crates were shaped like coffins, or more appropriately caissons, and into them went fishing rods, hunting and riding gear, and in the center amidst blankets and puffs Mama's Dresden teacups.

One year somehow a frog jumped in and jumped out again in Boston while Papa was unnailing the thing. It

103

startled Mama so, we had to fly for her smelling salts, but Papa laughed and said he'd fix frog's legs for supper.

One final day that I remember well, from 5 A.M. until the ferry left at seven, the house sounded like a train yard with engines backing and filling as it made up its cars. Papa was not with us; he'd left a few days before on urgent business at Tufts — blessed Tufts. But Professor James was with us, due to a badly sprained ankle he could hardly step on when Papa left.

Finally after a scrappy meal in which the plates were grabbed away to be washed before one had rightly finished (anyway it was sheer waste for Mama and the "girls" to eat), the funeral cortege, as I thought of it, began to form in the driveway in front of the house. Mama went out to look at it, gave a little scream, and swooned backwards into Professor James's arms.

At first I thought it was the sight of the yellow-wheeled democrat to which Pompey and Caesar were harnessed, leading the procession, that startled her so. But I guess it wasn't that; it was James Fox holding the reins. Instead of his gray whipcord livery and high derby hat, he'd cut loose from them with a vengeance.

A yatching cap sat jauntily above his red, shining, freshly shaven face peppered plentifully with twirls of toilet paper over many bleeding nicks from his razor. A white shirt billowed in the breeze, held in place with wide scarlet suspenders. The shirt cuffs covered his ungloved hands allowing only the black fingernails to show. Bright sky-blue pants terminated the costume, their coat lying beside him on the seat.

How Professor James laughed as he whispered words of

comfort. "It isn't Commonwealth Avenue, Alice. You have only to drive to the ferry, and most people are asleep anyway at this outlandish hour. But look behind James, I beg of you, at your daughter's handiwork.

"Oh, Punkin, Punkin," he said to me as his eye fell on Shimmo, who was tied behind the democrat in full mourning, saddled and bridled with my riding boots back-to in the stirrups.

I had never seen Professor James so tickled as his eyes traveled down the line. Behind Shimmo came Lowell, our caretaker, driving his box wagon drawn by the "colt," who had been called a colt for twenty years and was knock-kneed now with age. In the box wagon sat the "girls," very solemn in anticipation of the sea voyage they dreaded. Each "girl" held the inevitable bagged cat, now in badly faded law-bags, the result of frequent washings because of their misdemeanors.

Then behind them came the crates on the jigger, drawn by the Town's horses loaned us by the Watering-Cart authorities to haul our load to the ferry. An account of all this would appear in the next issue of the *Inquirer & Mirror*, in which Papa was referred to always as "Doc. Williams."

Malcolm then came cheerfully galloping up on his pony to station himself as postillion beside his scowling Mama.

"Why he and not Punkin too?" asked the Professor.

"Oh," replied Mama feebly, "that. In his best suit, deciding to have one last nostalgic slide down the barn roof, he caught on a nail. You can see the cloth waving its farewell from here, as it parted company with the rest of the trousers. So we had to scramble about and get him into riding breeches. Oh Lud, William, these trips are truly devastating." ("Lud" was her favorite curse word.)

Never in my life had I seen Professor James so truly animated or so shaking with suppressed laughter.

James, Shimmo, and I were first to reach the wharf. The captain of the ferry was standing on the bridge ordering the loading. When the men tried to lift the crates off the jigger which was backed up as close as it could get without drowning, he whistled and called out, "Say boys, get Mrs. Williams and her maids bedded first — then all hands lift them hefty tonnage freights aboard."

We reconnoitered at Woods Hole and got on the train, Mama, sick as she was, casting furtive glances about in case Lizzie Fay might be in the offing and behold her coachman who was everywhere at once and frightfully busy loading his horses. She looked woefully unhappy, so much so that Malcolm, trying to get into her good graces, asked solicitously, "Do you feel trainsick, Mama dear, or are you still seasick?"

She glared at him. "This is one of the times I regret not having taken the veil," she said, and this time Professor James burst out laughing.

As the train left the Back Bay station on its way to the last stop, Mama turned to Professor James and said, "I'll bid you goodbye now, William, for I simply will not drive up Commonwealth Avenue in our carriage, past Major Higginson's house — in broad daylight too — in that outfit of James's. I'd look like part of Barnum & Bailey and I will *not*."

Then she added, "Oh, I beg your pardon!" for she had stamped violently on his foot instead of on the floor.

We Move to Boston in the Fall

"All right, Alice, I can understand. You and I will take a cab. I'll get out at the Harvard Bridge and take the trolley to Cambridge," he said soothingly.

Mama, complacent that the trip home from the station in the cab with Professor James had rightly severed any connection between crimson-suspendered James Fox and her own unfortunate alliance with the Williams family, was doomed to receive a shock.

At a dinner party some time later what should fall upon her ears (as she was lifting a bit of crabmeat to her lips) but the voice of Major Higginson, to which all present were listening in rapt attention. What that voice was saying caused the bit of crabmeat to plunge down into her bosom! It was a detailed account of James Fox, red suspenders, Pompey and Caesar, a yellow democrat, two handsome Puerto Rican ponies led behind—and a dark-haired boy that looked very much like Harold's youngest son riding one of them.

"Really a comical sight," he laughed, "too early for the circus, but it's never out of season for one of Harold's displays!"

After reaching home and retrieving the crabmeat, Mama, with a frigid look at Papa, acted the part of a deaf and dumb person until an invitation to dinner came for them both from Major and Mrs. Higginson. They drove to dinner behind James Fox, who wore livery of a demure shade as he soberly handled Pompey and Caesar. Mama was in her most charming mood and by coincidence crabmeat was served again, but this time it found its proper goal.

19

The Year of the Spider

TAKING UP the tracks on the water side of Beacon Street only caused the wooden block pavement in front of our house to rise, and then, as the Esplanade was being constructed behind our house, rats and spiders by the millions made tracks into all basements on our block. It was truly a plague.

Sometimes while sitting reading peacefully of an evening before the library fire, Papa deep in Sir Walter Scott and Mama indulging in a mild, pleasant novel with no murders, insanity, or lack of breeding allowable in it, we would all be startled by her leap and yelp.

"Papa, come quickly. A spider's crawling up my back!" And he, forced to leave Mary, Queen of Scots, in the arms of Quentin, would unfasten her dress and peer down. There being no spider, he would sigh, return to the beautiful queen, and Mama, consoled for the moment, would go on with "little Polly picking buttercups" or something of the sort. Mama had the strangest method of reading — between a whisper and full voice. One could hear her "fits-feesing" all over the place, and suddenly she would put on the brakes and examine a fingernail in deep concentration before taking up the refrain again. Perhaps it had some connection with that "finishing" school (so aptly named) where pronunciation was all-important. She never reclined, either, but always sat bolt upright, as walking about with a book on her head had been a major part of that school's curriculum.

The cats on our block were hardly prepared to cope with the invasion, having had little to do but sit on their high back fences and pass the time of day. The alley was traversed only by delivery and garbage trucks before the innovation of the Esplanade turned our alley into a Champs Elysées.

In a house at one end of the block lived Dr. Louisa Paine Tingley, who had two cats, Horace and Pauline. Dr. Tingley was an oculist and graduate of Tufts. Papa, coming home from the Medical School into the blasting wind of Charlesgate East, would frequently have something fly into his eye and he'd visit her, weeping buckets.

"You've not enough eyelashes, Dr. Williams," she'd comment severely after attending to that pitiful orb before whose stern glance she had often quailed in the classroom.

Next door to her lived the famous tuberculosis specialist, Dr. Vincent Bowditch, owner of a stunning white cat, Puff Ball, known to all of us as "Puff Ball Bowditch." Then came of course our retinue of five, led by Jeremiah Williams. Next door lived a maker of Pippin cigars who sported a thoroughbred Angora cat, by far the most patrician on the block. As for the man himself, Mama was mightily displeased at being called "dearie" and having her arm squeezed as they met in the doorway.

At the other end of our street lived Tom Lawson, a very rich copper king. He had no cats, but high-stepping, prize-winning, dock-tailed cobs whom he named after his five daughters, each cob's name prefaced by the word "Glorious." The one I remember was Glorious Bunny.

With mammoth dredging and truck dumping of earth, the Esplanade grew and the Charles River retreated. The incursions of rats and spiders kept the cat population overworked. I think actually Mama and Jeremiah suffered most, though from slightly different causes, but each got similar medicinal aid from Papa.

"A fortieth of a grain, Mama dear" (strychnine, I believe) and "Control yourself, Jeremiah, my boy, while I put this nice restorative in your fish."

Jeremiah one day corralled seven rats in the back yard by standing guard at the only exit hole. But as he pounced on one, not having time to kill it, the next sly one would near the exit and require a pounce in turn. As finally they all escaped with only battle scars, he threw himself spread-eagled on the bricks exhausted, and Papa, who had been proudly watching from a window, hurried down with the strychnine. Back again with more dosage for Mama, who sat clenching the arms of her chair and shrieking as a large black spider slowly descended before her very nose.

It was a very trying winter. Dinner was late one night and Papa tried to keep the cause a secret from us as he galloped to the kitchen with the aromatic spirits. Edith the cook was prostrate and sprawled on a chair. Apparently as she trekked between stove and icebox, her foot barely missed two swollen, drowned rats. To show her bravado before the other girls, who were feeling faint, Edith had put on gloves and essayed to pick up the rats and hurl them afar, when both tails came off in her gloved hands. She too nearly lost consciousness, at least all consciousness of serving dinner.

Uncle Mort lived on the next block and suffered equally. One day while he was writing his new book he glanced up and saw two beady black eyes watching him, their rodent owner sitting on a treatise entitled *Nerve Variations in Carnivore*. Uncle Mort told this with great pleasure, saying, "There was I struggling for an explanation while an authority on the subject sat looking at me in pity."

A few blocks nearer the State House lived Governor Draper, who roared to the legislature, "We've got to do away with rats and spiders for breakfast, dinner and supper, I tell you — Esplanade or no Esplanade!"

We found that "the water side of Beacon," no longer a prestigious place to live, was also no longer a meeting place for tea and conversation.

"We'll wait till you get to Nantucket, Alice dear," said Aunt Maud, who lived on the other side of Beacon Street which was unrodented and unspidered.

"Summer'll soon be here," said the three Professors, who lived in Cambridge.

"You really can't blame them," said Mama, drinking her tea with a watchful eye and getting up for a good shake every few minutes.

No man-manipulated scheme caused the final exodus and I've no idea to what country they migrated — but eventually all was calm again. And on the truly beautiful Esplanade could be seen Papa, flanked by Cardinal O'Connell and Dr. Van Allen of the Church of the Advent, taking their afternoon sprint as if never a rat nor spider had ever been seen there.

20

Cleopatra

"DR. PRINCE, please sir, put on your trousers. Your patient Mrs. Bellamy will be here in fifteen minutes for her appointment." Kody was speaking urgently.

"Blast Mrs. Bellamy, Kody. Get Dr. Williams on the telephone right away. Who is Mrs. Bellamy? Not that jackass who has a compulsive urge to jump into the Charles River in January? Never mind, get Dr. Williams and let her go to the devil!"

"Yes, sir, but you're in your briefs, sir."

Uncle Mort stationed himself, legs apart firmly, before Kody and spoke.

"Don't you realize, Kody, that it's imperative I get Dr. Williams and try to stop him being eaten by Cleopatra before it's too late?"

"I don't recall your mentioning the lady, sir. Here are your trousers, Dr. Prince."

113

"Kody, you're an ass. Get Dr. Williams," pulling on his trousers.

"Yes, sir. The line is busy, sir."

"Oh thunder! Well, keep trying. You know, Kody, I've been writing Dr. Williams's obituary? Nice ending it will be if I can't stop him from this latest act of insanity: 'Dr. Harold Williams, dean of Tufts Medical, was most unfortunately killed and totally eaten today by Cleopatra at Barnum & Bailey's Circus. In consideration of her (he worships animals) he did not wear his pink tights or ostrich plume as he did in his spectacular event, for fear of causing Cleopatra laryngitis as he tended her medically, in case she didn't cooperate. A memorial service will be held at Emmanuel Church, which he does not attend, but of which he is a member. As no physical evidence such as a coffin and pall bearers can be present, due to his somewhat unusual demise, friends are requested not to send flowers.'

"Or do you think, Kody, we should have a voodoo sort of ceremony, with a dance around the funeral pyre for the dear departed, who is, after all, inside Cleopatra, and thus let the flames consume both of them? What do you think?"

Kody at the telephone turned to Uncle Mort calmly. "Perhaps, sir, if I knew what you were talking about I could answer better. Here is Dr. Williams on the line and Mrs. Bellamy is ringing the door bell, sir."

"All right, get my trousers."

"Yes sir, you're in them, sir."

"Oh, so I am. Harold, you're not going through with this?" — into the telephone.

Papa's answer over the wire: "Of course I am, but don't

114

say anything to Alice. That glorious, intelligent, magnificent tigress has a fistula that must be opened. Why, she's refusing to nurse her two little cubs even, she's in such agony."

"Harold, who's going to nurse the poor little dean?"

"Don't be an ass, Mort. Mind my office till I get back. Be acting dean for me, Mort."

"And you call me lopsided mentally, Harold? Well, I know there's no stopping you. Farewell, friend of many years," and Uncle Mort hung up.

"No, Kody," he said to the manservant who was handing him a cup of coffee, "I'll never eat again, man, if anything happens to Dr. Williams."

"It does sound a bit dangerous, sir," said Kody mildly.

"*Dangerous* — it's suicidal, Kody, you idiot!"

"Yes, sir. Mrs. Bellamy, sir."

Uncle Mort was pacing the floor and chewing his mustache furiously. "Open the window on the river, Kody, and lead her to it."

"Yes, sir," said Kody, going to the door and saying courteously, "This way, Mrs. Bellamy, please. Dr. Prince is in his office." And opening the office door he added, "Here is Mrs. Bellamy, Dr. Prince."

Meanwhile Papa was readying himself for the encounter. Barnum & Bailey Circus had their tents pitched very near Tufts Medical on Huntington Avenue and, like a schoolboy playing truant, the Dean had made constant secret forays and thus had discovered Cleopatra's ailment. It fascinated him to feed peanuts to the elephants, even when one, wrapping his trunk around him, swung him onto the plateau of his back and then walked about, refusing to put him down again. That day he was late for his heart lecture.

The monkeys, of course, were so charming to Papa that playing with them made him lose track of time, and the dean's office secretaries, Miss Lillian or Miss Chandler, had to gallop after him and become severe.

To return to Cleopatra, Papa on this awesome day stood before her cage, medicine bag in hand and wearing a discarded coat of her keeper's in order to have a more friendly smell. Four guards with rifles trained on the tigress were positioned around the quadrangular cage. Of those rifles he was indeed afraid, but not in the least of Cleopatra.

The beautiful great beast lay moaning in a corner, her swollen, aching paw extended in front of her. Two very young cubs cowered in a further corner, having all too often endured Mama's cuffings when they drew near for their sustenance.

Firmly he opened the cage door and stood just inside it as it clanged behind him. She raised her head and looked at him with large, cold, green eyes that told him nothing.

Slowly, very quietly he walked towards her, carrying his medicine bag. She raised her upper lip, exposing the tremendous fangs sharpened to a point, but though growling softly she allowed him to approach. Holding her eyes, he very slowly kneeled down before her. This too she allowed, smelling the hand he raised to stroke her beautiful head while he talked softly to her, telling her of his sympathy. Her whiskers twitched as she continued her "smelling" inspection of his arm, the coat, the medicine bag, while always the green cold eyes never left his face.

Then he felt secure in lifting the great swollen paw and resting it on his knee. She moaned, but allowed it. Next he took out his scalpel from the medicine bag and let her smell it. Holding it over the fistula for a brief second he felt his nerves quiver because he heard four rifles click. But he banished the momentary fear and whispered aloud, "I'm going to save your life, Cleo — help me." With a quick, deep slash he opened the abcess and closed his eyes as a stream of pus flew out. The tigress roared and sprang to her feet, whirling about the cage in agony. The roar lessened, became a whine, then limping she returned to the same spot, lay down, and rested her eyes again upon his. Petting her a moment, he then reached in the medicine bag, drew forth and uncorked a large bottle of iodine — this too she smelled — and then he poured the entire contents into the bleeding, oozing wound.

She moaned and quivered down the whole vast length of her beautiful striped back. A bandage and drain next (this also had to be smelled and it took several lengths of bandage for her great paw), then he was finished.

Papa later said he had hated to leave — they had a distinct rapport which he strongly felt — and he was tremendously impressed with her intelligence. She smelled each implement of torture to be sure, but the rapport went further than that confirmation: she trusted him to wield those implements.

He stroked her and talked to her a few moments, to the extreme agitation of the gunners, who still expected reprisals in a lightning pounce. Then he backed out of the cage. And for all his bravado, the first thing he did was to light a cigarette.

In less than an hour Cleopatra turned on her side and gave that "prrr" sound we hear in pleased kitties. The cubs wobbled over to her and she let them nurse.

Mama read the account that night in the *Transcript*, the first she had heard of the incident, and the eye she fastened upon Papa was as cold as Cleopatra's.

"I suppose, Papa, I should be grateful at not seeing your name amongst the deaths when you handed me that page of the paper. But really! And you call Mort lopsided mentally, Papa. Must I live my entire life through imagining widowhood and our children orphaned?"

He laughed. "Well, Mama dear, at least you won't be afraid of spiders any more when you think of my tigress and me holding hands. You know you should have come in the cage with me and cured your spider fears for all time."

She tossed her head. "I don't pretend to know much history, but it was my impression that Cleopatra was not especially partial to ladies."

The episode has an epilogue. The circus came back two years later. Papa was let off Mama's apron string after a solemn promise not to go into the cage if Cleopatra happened to be in the circus troupe.

There were several cages of tigers and tigresses. Papa didn't recognize Cleopatra — but suddenly one beautiful, gleaming, striped tigress raised her head, sniffed, twitched her whiskers and then gamboled, rolled over and over, purred loudly, and rolled some more.

Who needs words, when they have that kind of intelligence!

21

The Supernatural Again

WHO CAN BE SURE which winter it was, but the Christmas box that Miss Gulielma Folger always sent us from Nantucket was delayed because of the ferocious weather. We were still celebrating after New Year's when it came and brightened a dark winter afternoon at teatime.

It always had a present for each of us and an extra packet for Papa of his favorite hard candy, called "Gentleman's Tears." And after we read her note — he needed them! It read:

"An extraordinary occurrence has taken place on the island. We now have a Mystic or a Medium or some strange creature: His name is Matthew Macy, native born, exiled for forty-odd years, returned last summer incognito to his homeland, and emerged before us for the first time this fall.

"Some folks say he was shanghaied out of New Bedford

on a whaler as a mere lad — he says nothing. We never knew he was on the island all last summer doing his ground work, until this October he began building himself a little house on that wild deserted moor of Tom Nevers Head and set up hermit housekeeping.

"Now, straighten your ears! He must have been the one who summoned you, Dr. Williams, the night Mary Murray's appendix kicked up; no one on the island knew a thing about it and Joe Murray was in such a stew he didn't know what to do for help and nearly dropped dead with astonishment when you appeared. Now, then, the following I don't believe, but I have to believe it!

"One foggy night at Sankaty Lighthouse the keeper and his wife were both too ill to climb the stairs and light the light. No one in the village could see it wasn't lit, because of the fog. And you know there are no neighbors. Well, Matthew Macy came clear across island and tended it all night! Tie that!

"I met him in the village buying a sack of flour and asked him bold as brass what that long low building was he was putting up near his little house. He looked at me and I tell you his eyes glow like stars.

" 'It's a horse barn,' he says, real quiet. 'I hope to board the summer people's horses, winters.'

"So there you have it, my dear Williamses, and won't this make Professors James and Taussig jealous that Dr. Prince has an edge on them now that he owns a house on the island.

"Happy New Year. Elma."

"Pass the 'Gentleman's Tears'," laughed Papa. "What an untoward happening!"

"For us it makes Nantucket a complete Nirvana," said all three of our scientists in chorus, while Mama and Aunt Maud pretended to shiver.

"Well, it spoils the island for me unless I can keep out of the bugger's way," said Papa. "You remember, Mama, years and years ago when we were trying to decide which it should be, Nantucket or Mount Desert? Of course Bishop Lawrence is at Bar Harbor, which tends to a pretty heavy religious atmosphere for me, as he's such a friend of brother Moses he'd feel obliged to keep an eye on me, but by George this is worse!"

But I could see him smile and chuckle as he did when he was joking. And I hasten to add that there was no hard feeling involved between my fiery father and the good Bishop, as was later demonstrated by his offer to officiate at my father's funeral — which he did.

22

The Hermit

TOM NEVERS HEAD in Nantucket was a wild, uninhabited stretch of moors. It held a peculiar fascination for Malcolm and me and we very cautiously skirted the high blueberry bushes on our ponies, our wooden daggers at our belts, seeking the "head" of Tom Nevers — an old Indian, it was said. When we learned that what we searched for was really only a promontory named for him, we threw away our wooden daggers in disgust.

Now there was a mystery about Tom Nevers Head, for a Hermit claimed his inheritance in the spot, and came back to it after years of travel. Malcolm and I promised each other that someday when we were in Nantucket, we would find him. So one day we did.

The stretch of land bordered a wide sweep of the Atlantic as far as the eye could see, and both the ocean and the moors were held in a sinister shadow of foreboding by the islanders, which accounted probably for its uninhabited desolation. A hotel had been built on the water's edge. It burned down. Fishermen had capsized and drowned in the treacherous currents and heavy undertow. All but Matthew Macy had walked away from Tom Nevers Head. It suited him.

Approaching, we saw a horse and gig leaving the compound and heading for the village, so when it disappeared from view we rode in, dismounted, and entered the long barn to hitch our ponies. As our eyes adjusted to the darker light, we were both startled to see all Ten Commandments painted in large letters on a dead white wall.

"Jeepers," said my brother, backing out, and I followed, a queer feeling in the back of my neck.

We did not speak. Hens, so tame they pecked at our riding boots, fussed and cackled in the barnyard, and some few milk goats nuzzled their soft noses in our palms. Walking towards the little house, we passed an enormous vegetable garden.

Malcolm went on to investigate the house while I approached the cliff on which the house stood. Never had I seen so lonely and sinister a spot. The cliff was high above the sea, and the sea was directly below it, with only a tiny bit of beach.* I pictured winter storms and gales when the hungry breakers would reach up to engulf and claim the little house and, because they could not, fall back defeated in a spewing green cascade. What kind of person

* In the past seventy years erosion on other parts of the island has given this small beach an added 600 feet of sand.

would choose this awesome place to live? I shivered. Malcolm had tried the kitchen door and found it unlocked. I joined him and we entered.

A kettle sang on the stove. Careless or intentional? We lifted a lid and found a dying fire, so guessed return of the owner was imminent; he surely would not risk his kettle. A tortoiseshell cat on a rocking chair yawned and stretched.

There was a large window facing the magnificent sweep of ocean and drawn up to it an old Morris chair, its torn lining forming a pocket for some bills of money and old letters. Wanting to go closer to look out the window at the stupendous view, more impressive from this height, I found myself detouring around the center table, which held a large open Bible on one end, a candlestick beside it; the candle burned low. Why, I wondered as I gave wide berth to the table, does Holy Writ give us this sense of awe? Must be "sin-pricks" bothering my conscience I told myself, and I hadn't far to look, for one old brown letter from the Morris chair was already in my hand!

And then the door opened. I wheeled, the letter, still unopened. There, filling the entire doorway, was — *John the Baptist*. It must be he, my reeling brain assured me, for it was an exact replica of the picture in our nursery Bible. Immense in stature, with a mop of rumpled hair and heavy black beard, dressed in the identical black smock that fell below the knees, they were the same, only this figure carried a sack of flour on his shoulder.

Frozen into immobility, I managed to glance towards Malcolm, who had crept behind the stove and was staring wide-eyed at the doorway. In my flying brain I found myself turning the page in our nursery Bible to gaze on Salome holding high above her head the gory dripping platter, and my knees gave way. Then he spoke quietly, reassuringly. It was the voice I had heard the night of Mrs. Captain Murray's operation, when the blast of our ox-horn had swept eerily through the house.

"Malcolm," he said, "reach into that cupboard above your head for the teapot and three cups," and as he spoke he set the sack of flour on the floor and came towards me. He lifted down from a shelf above my head a canister of tea. That this canister had painted upon it dragons, reptiles, and tigers was not conducive to reassurance, but his eyes resting on me were. Brilliant dark eyes that seemed to look through me, as very quietly he took the letter from my shaking hand and put it back in the lining of the old chair. Then he put an enormous hand on my head and said softly, "Come, children, we'll have a cup of tea. It's very good tea. I brought it from China home with me."

There was a rhythm in that deep, slow voice, like the waves breaking on a beach, that soothed me so I could drink my tea. Malcolm felt it too, he told me later. In spite of my guilt I was quite comfortable.

"You may take this canister of tea home to your mother with my compliments," he murmured. "I have plenty more." He stood up, but I knew I had a job to do so I tackled it as best I could.

"I didn't read your letter, sir," I faltered, "though I guess I meant to all right. I — I'm sorry."

He looked into my eyes so long it made my heart beat, but I knew I mustn't drop mine. How his eyes did glow — Miss Folger was right.

"I forgive you, child," he said. "I don't think you'll do

it again, perhaps never again." Then he opened the door for us.

"I never tasted such delicious tea," said Mama at supper. "We must drive out and thank him, Papa."

"We?" grunted my father. "You go, you know how I abominate these visionaries."

"But not their tea," she replied. "Do you realize you're on your fifth cup?"

"Quite unthinking, Mama dear. I am completely absorbed in my thoughts."

"Is he really John the Baptist, Papa, come back again?" I asked.

"Is he *what?* Oh, for heaven's sake, lamb chop, go to bed."

23

Professor Pickering

I THINK it was a special cycle of the moon which so intensely interested Professor Pickering. At first he used to frighten me when I was sometimes taken along on moonlight nights. He set up his tripod telescope on an unobstructed stretch of the moors and became a Mephistophelean object in my eyes — skull cap, flowing black cape, legs wide apart, torso rigidly bent forward — as he pointed his telescope in intense concentration on the heavens. The tides absorbed his days, and by daylight I recovered, as Malcolm and I tagged along to "help" on his calculations. He was really amazingly kind, allowing me to carry the pencil while Malcolm commandeered the notebook.

This was one of the best known of our friends listed in *Dan's Dictionary*, where even Uncle Mort is not mentioned. Dan quotes him as being an astronomer, calls him "Edward Charles Pickering," and dates him 1846–1919. He was a quiet, gentle person, first discovered by my mother on one of the trips my parents took through the Berkshires each autumn on Mr. Bert Bigelow's coach and four. How such a reticent man got to be one of this rollicking, jolly party I can't answer, for in the evenings around the fire, after they left the tally-ho and put up at the Red Lion Inn or another similar one, he sat apart and was a silent onlooker until my mother drew him out — and in. Professor Pickering fast became one of our group of friends, even graduating as Malcolm's godfather.

I had a personal gripe on the subject of godparents, mine being my father (whom I had anyway), and a fussy, tiresome little old aunt who wore a bonnet with a bird on it, a perennial bonnet enduring into my teens with the bird doctored up and regilded each spring. That little bird told her, no doubt, that for colds we children got a teaspoonful of whiskey in sugared hot water, and that is why for my Christmas present every year from her I drew a bottle of whiskey and a five-dollar gold piece (one taken immediately away from me and the other banked), while Malcolm got for his Christmas presents real and lavish ones from Professor Pickering. Perhaps the Professor's constant use of the Harvard Observatory increased his powers of observation, for I was eventually included among the recipients of his Christmas presents.

One day Uncle Mort, partially recovered from his intense, probing study of strange personalities, revived his interest in Matthew Macy, the mystic, and made a suggestion to Professor Pickering.

"Edward, you old boot, I say, what if I ask Harold for

the parrot horse — he says the currents and shoals are critical at Tom Nevers — and we go and see. I don't know mine yet well enough to take one."

Professor Pickering scowled, then laughed.

"Mort," he said, "do your students *really* ever know what you're talking about? I'll accept anyway; I'd like to hear a horse talk."

"Thunder," said Uncle Mort and chewed his mustache. "Kody!" he then shouted, "go and ask Dr. Williams if we can borrow the parrot horse; we can use our own runabout."

"Yes, sir," said Kody, "but our own Winifred is very tractable, Michael says."

"No, I don't want anything to do with her."

"Very good, sir," and Kody left.

We ran for our ponies to accompany this expedition.

When we told Papa later he smiled. "Your Uncle Mort and the parrot horse are mentally attuned," he said. "He *never* balks for him. Seriously though, many people believe it is a mental block that makes a horse balk. If so, Uncle Mort understands him."

We arrived at Matthew Macy's at a nice fast clip, the parrot horse's ears forward as always when Uncle Mort held the reins. Malcolm and I loitered near while Professor Pickering knocked on the kitchen door. It was opened at once by the tall black-smocked figure of the Hermit.

"My name is Pickering, Mr. Macy. I'm an astronomer, and this is Dr. Prince. I have heard the sea in front of your house here abounds in reefs and shoals, and if you'll permit me I'd like to make some calculations."

After the customary long look and pause, the heavy-bearded lips parted in a smile. Showing big white teeth, he replied quietly, "The sea belongs to us all, Professor Pickering. Certainly, feel quite free."

Uncle Mort here pushed forward.

"I'm a psychologist, Macy," he blurted out, "and am tremendously interested in these rumored premonitions of yours. May I come in and talk to you right now?"

An arm went up barring entrance, the large figure stiffened, and the voice that replied cut like ice across all our ears.

"You must excuse me, Dr. Prince, if I refuse to speak of these matters to you now or at any time." And he shouldered past both men and walked towards the barn.

"You're too precipitate, Mort," said the Professor. "Remember this is a recluse, unused to your explosive manner. I'm sorry, old man," as Uncle Mort looked so chastened and disappointed.

"I'd looked forward to it so and now when you leave the island I've no excuse at all to ever come for another try. The man is poison to Harold; he'd never bring me."

"I'll put in a word, though I doubt its efficacy," said Professor Pickering, and he went to the barn where he too was temporarily put off balance by the large, imposing presence of the Ten Commandments. A horse was being curried by the Hermit in its stall.

"Dr. Prince is most apologetic for offending you, Mr. Macy, and he begged me to tell you." Professor Pickering spoke gently.

The currycomb stopped working for a moment, then impulsively the Hermit spoke as he looked over the horse's back at Professor Pickering.

Professor Pickering

"Is it true that Professor William James is going to visit Dr. Williams with his friend Professor Taussig? The children have just mentioned it to me." He spoke rather eagerly.

"Yes," replied the Professor, who was a bit surprised at the question. "We will all be here at the time of the harvest moon. Dr. Prince is one of our group, a very cherished one I may add, as is also Miss Maud Howe, Mrs. Julia Ward Howe's daughter."

Matthew Macy put down his currycomb and came out of the stall. He was smiling.

"I should like to meet Professor James, for I have news of a European friend of his he would be glad to hear. I met this man in India; he was living with the yogis when I too was with them." He put up his hand. "After that meeting — Dr. Prince," and he kept on smiling.

"James always cuts in ahead of me," growled Uncle Mort when he heard of this. "So be it then, at the time of the harvest moon. I will just have to wait. The yogis — hmm."

And so the summer rolled pleasantly along, with plans for the reunion of our friends, which Matthew Macy suggested include an oyster supper at his place, anxious as he was to meet Professor James and an "R" being in the month of September. And we children were to get the oysters from our own bed at Monomoy!

[24]

The County Fair

"I DIDN'T KNOW Professor Pickering had a dog," I remarked to Malcolm as we sat smoking sweet-fern cigarettes in the hayloft one rainy day.

"I don't know about his private life much when he's away from us, only his public life with us."

"Well, that's enough, I guess. He surely brings good presents," I said contentedly.

"I wonder what kind of a dog it is; his name is Star and he calls him that, Dog-Star. He must be a pretty fine dog."

"Is he going to put him for showing in the County Fair, do you suppose?" said Malcolm. "Lord, I can hardly wait for the day to come."

A heavy step sounded and James Fox lumbered up the ladder.

"Holy creepin' saints!" he ejaculated. "*Smokin'* be ye, young varmints, and in the hay! Come down outa there this exact minute. If Papa sees this, neither one o' you will be able to walk for a week for the whalin's you'll get."

"All right, all right — I guess it is a little risky," said Malcolm irritably as James took both our cigarettes and pinched them out.

"Do you know, James, if the other professors are coming for the County Fair?"

"Aye, the lot, and Miss Maud too."

"Jeepers," said Malcolm.

"Some is stayin' at your Uncle Mort's, Michael says," went on James, herding us down.

"Where's the dog staying?" I asked, but I got no answer as James said, "Hand me the matches, little Alice, this exact minute."

They arrived all together. Professor James was very tired from a series of lectures and thought the County Fair would relax him. Malcolm and I went to the ferry to meet them.

"What are the children up to?" I heard Professor James ask Papa. "I noticed Punkin peering all around our legs as we got off the boat."

"Heaven knows," laughed Papa. "Why such a good law-abiding man as I should have such a pair of brats always doing the unexpected I'll never know."

"Chip off the old block, Harold, I guess," said the Professor. "I must question Punkin."

Next day was the fair, long awaited. We were up at five, each clutching our whole dollar bill Papa'd given us and envisioning a day without any sign of a leash, a day Papa had prescribed for us. With our harnessed ponies we arrived at the fair grounds before the ticket taker was there — and thus saved twenty-five cents of our dollar. We took up residence under a wagon full of hay for the race horses, to plan our strategy.

By nine o'clock when the influx of people had started, I had eaten most of my dollar and had to consider replenishing it. A great many of the vendors had come from the Cape; one had a booth of the most delectable chipped beef, hot and buttery on a bun. To him I offered my services, suggesting, "Could I wear that placard round my neck and that tall white hat and walk around advertising for you?"

"Why sure, little snookums," he replied. "Good idea."

"How much?" I asked, firmly gripping the remaining nickel in my pocket.

"Oh, a dollar, I guess, cutie."

Off I went, jubilant, on my rounds.

I didn't show much of me, done up in the hat which was too big and came way down and the huge placard covering my front. It read: "Come and get a bun, hot and fine with chipped beef. Such 'nuritchin' food." But as Papa and Mama walked into the fair grounds, he took one horrified glance and said urgently to Mama, "Look, isn't that Mrs. Estes?" Then taking her arm, he steered her away from me.

I lost Malcolm; my exchequer newly replenished, I had a burst of sisterly love, knowing how impoverished he must be, and went in search of him. I found him at the "dog house," making arrangements for Professor Pickering's dog, he said. He wanted to be sure there was a ring for him to be tied on, and paid all of forty cents to hold it.

"Get a receipt," I said, "idiot."

So, after seeing "Dog-Star Pickering" pinned up over the ring, we left.

The County Fair

It was so gorgeous — flags, banners, crowds of milling people, booths of popcorn, lightship baskets, little tiny shells with scenes painted in them like Sankaty Light, the ferry, and the Oldest House, all for sale.

One booth had a big tank with a swordfish in it, for twenty-five cents per look. He looked to me as if he needed a reviving dose of strychnine from Papa.

There was a fortune-teller lady in another booth, who smelled awful and was all covered with rings and jangles and a red handkerchief over her head. James and Michael were in the race horse tent, betting. James bet on Genevieve, the trotter belonging to Captain Remson, but Michael said no, the fish-market horse Further More would win.

Papa kept driving our four-wheeled yellow democrat to collect people who didn't have carriages. He got old Miss Sheffield who kept the candy store; she parted her hair in the middle and wore a tortoise shell comb in the back of it and always kissed us (wet), spoiling the anticipation of the candy we went for. Then he went for Billy Clark, the town crier, who dressed himself up like a clown and sold knickknacks. Lastly he called at the poorhouse and got the two little orphans, Fred and Ted; they were all clean and starched, dressed in two Peter Thompsons Malcolm had outgrown.

Before the horse racing began Malcolm and I took a couple of naps together under the hay wagon. I'd given him part of my last dollar because I was a little too full of chipped beef and he felt likewise from an overdose of popcorn.

When the bell rang, we rushed for the rope. Off they

135

went, Further More in the lead but Genevieve pushing her, James and Michael yelling their heads off and jumping up and down.

"Will you stop leaping on me pet corn, you great lubber of an Irishman?" cried James, holding his injured foot in his hand and hopping on the other. "Hooray-ha-ha, me Genevieve is won!" as the bell clanged and Captain Remson, behind her in the sulky, grinned his face off.

They put a wreath around Genevieve's neck as she stood panting, and people crowded about the Captain, shaking his hand and slapping him on the back. Suddenly a tall, spare figure in a foulard dress with large flowers on it (flowers that never grew on land or sea) and a hat with a bird in front, a streamer behind, approached. This was Mrs. Captain Remson. Kissing Genevieve on the nose, she went then to the captain and, with eyes starry with joy, laid her hand on his arm and said in a choking voice, "It's wonderful, Gibby — but remember the light. The sun is setting; we must get going." His face snapped into earnestness. The light that shone far out to sea from the Sankaty Lighthouse, the light was their charge, their duty, and their life. Raising his hand to the crowd, he moved himself to a seat out on the shafts, handed Mrs. Captain Remson into the sulky seat, and with Genevieve still in her wreath they turned eastward to the call of duty.

It was time to go home at last — all of us in different carriages. Mama, driven by James in the yellow-wheeled democrat, had little Fred and Ted, exhausted and all sticky with candy, and in the back seat, listing against her as he dozed off, the poor old tired clown in his gruesome mask. Papa had Miss Sheffield in the runabout with him, while

The County Fair

I took Professor James with Shimmo in the buggy, and Malcolm had Professor Pickering in a box wagon drawn by his pony. He also took the popcorn man and the "nuritchin" chipped beef man, who infuriated him by saying, "You ain't as smart as your little sister, little man, be ye?"

We all had supper at our house. Malcolm kept making faces at me. I knew what he meant and obliged.

"Professor Pickering, where was your dog?" I asked.

"What dog, little Alice?" he asked, surprised.

"Why, Dog-Star, of course. Didn't you come to visit us this time, Professor Pickering, on purpose to put him in the County Fair?"

Shouts of laughter around the supper table.

"I can hardly credit my ears," Professor James was shaking. "Punkin, however do you think of such things?"

"Show them your receipt," I ordered Malcolm, "then Professor James will believe it."

The dirty, sticky paper was produced. It read, "Rec'd $.40 to reserve a ring in the wall to tie Dog-Star — owner, Pickering."

Again, a lot of laughter. Extraordinary to us how anyone could laugh over such a loss as forty cents.

Taken out onto the piazza by the two professors, we had "Dog Star" pointed out to us and were told it was particularly brilliant this night.

"At least it can hold itself up there," I remarked gloomily, "without a forty-cent expense."

We both felt pretty foolish, but that feeling eased up a bit when Professor Pickering reimbursed our financial loss.

Hypnotism Again Attacks Papa

A BLESSED LULL, so rare in our family, took place after Papa's and my second entrance into a Medical Journal, the editor of which I could have gladly locked in a closet for publishing it. This time, after an explicit rehearsal of motions from Papa, I extricated a fish hook from a screaming fisherman's eye. He later glared at me with that eye and called me a cold-blooded, brutal little monster. Professor James, on hearing of it, said to Papa (who agreed with the fisherman), "You praise suffocation of schoolmistresses, Harold, and expect tenderness?"

The lull extended to Malcolm and me, everyone else being busy with preparations for the Harvest Moon Celebration, now only three days hence. I lay in the hammock, reading and licking my chops as Carver Doone "limb by limb sank from sight" in the quicksand. Malcolm at that crucial and delightful moment howled up from the cubby house for the immediate loan of my big toe for electrical shock experiments he was conducting in competition with a Mr. Edison.

That night the lull ended. Our ox-horn gave its eerie shriek and old Jethro's niece called up to us: "Doctor, come quick! Uncle saw a rat's eyes gleaming in the dark in a corner of our cabin and crept out of bed to shoot it — but oh, Doc, he held one hand over the barrel. His hand is hangin' and awful bloody and he's a-yippin' and a-yappin' somethin' awful and jumpin' up and down."

I moaned and shook with rage clear to my toenails — but no, the brisk voice of Papa was telling Mama in the hall, "This is for Burrage, I'll go right after him, thank goodness he's on the island." I turned over.

Some days later, it was hard to tell which rat Papa was talking about, Dr. Burrage or the one with gleaming eyes, both came in for such a word-lashing. Apparently Dr. Burrage had claimed he could reattach the hanging fingers while Papa advocated amputation, and Jethro took a "hate" on Papa for suggesting it, so Dr. Burrage did his "embroidery" and promptly left the island, his vacation over. Then the gangrene set in and Papa took Uncle Mort with him, thank heaven, this time.

Old Jethro was in agony and lavish with curses when Papa said the hand must come off now at the elbow, as he saw the green snakelike poison creeping over the wrist. Papa was "rat angry" and said in no uncertain terms that he also had not one drop of ether left and that it would take two days to get a can from Boston even by telegram and, he added quietly, "We haven't got two days."

"You git outa here, you bald-headed old devil!" screamed

Jethro. "You ain't hog-tying and butcherin' me. Git!" My father went outside and walked up and down. Uncle Mort stayed inside with the yowling patient for almost an hour, then he came out and said to my pacing father, "Sit down, Harold, and don't explode at what I'm going to say. I think I can hypnotize him."

"But he won't have an amputation," cried Papa.

"Yes, he will — it's the pain he's afraid of. Now there was a case written up of a woodsman in West Virginia. A tree fell on his leg; a doctor was passing by in a buggy, hypnotized him, and amputated the leg."

Papa's face flushed, Uncle Mort said, and he clenched his fists and jaw and became livid.

"You're caught this time, Harold, between your Hippocratic oath and your darn-fool prejudices, old man. It's this or let the old cuss die."

How Harold did glare, Uncle Mort later told Mama, and again he paced up and down. Finally he spoke.

"I have no choice. Go in and put him to sleep, get the girl to boil the teakettle and my instruments and call me. He'll never go to sleep if he sees me." Then Papa muttered, "Why do these things have to happen to me?" and began the "rat chorus" again, in which Dr. Burrage took the prize.

It apparently worked. I was again in the hammock when we saw them coming up the road, Uncle Mort driving the parrot horse, Papa sitting beside him like a statue, his arms folded. Hurriedly I read over for the twentieth time: "Beautiful eyes, loving eyes, the sound of a shot rang through the church and those eyes were filled with death."

That moment Papa came stamping up the piazza steps

saying, "I'm going to bed, Mama. Please don't let anyone disturb me."

"Are you ill, Papa?" she asked anxiously.

"No," he said, "I just feel — *shot.*" And he left and Uncle Mort came up to Mama.

"Heavens," I thought, "everybody's getting shot — Papa, Jethro's rat, and Lorna Doone. Well, so what?" and I crept back to the hammock, lest Malcolm hear me moving about and call for my toe. Later I asked Mary for some "dipped toast," our remedy when ill, and took it to my father as he lay in his darkened room. "Ugh," he said, but patted my hand, and I tiptoed out.

Then I heard Uncle Mort say to Mama, "Harold had to come to grips with hypnotism, Alice. The old man groaned all the time but he didn't struggle and Harold did a fine job — the old cuss will be all right now. Heaven knows about Harold!"

"Don't tease him about it, Mort," said Mama. "He looked dreadfully shaken."

"I won't, though I must tell Professor James. Poor old Harold." And Uncle Mort went home.

[26]

Under the Harvest Moon

WITH MUCH CLATTERING of hooves and clanking of harness, five wagons full of merrymakers drew to a halt in the barnyard of the Hermit, who went — with unusual rapidity for him — to welcome them. A barrage of arguments began, principally about where to settle, for Aunt Fanny's maximum comfort. Finally it reached agreement. She would stay in her victoria, a fire would be made on the barnyard stones, blankets spread around it on the ground and "lapeating" employed. This settled, bedlam ensued, everyone flying into a chore, running into each other, shouting orders — like a flock of wild, honking geese.

"Let's get away from here," I said to Malcolm, and we went to the cliff overlooking the sea. The harvest moon was full, casting a dancing, shimmering path of radiance on the ocean, which around that path of light looked black and menacing in its slow, writhing movement. If fairies were dancing on that brilliant carpet path of moonlight, maybe they were singing too in voices too high for human ears, and the breakers booming on the beach gave them of their rhythm and provided an obligato for them. We were silent. Professor Pickering, a lone escapee, stood apart, his telescope pointed heavenwards, like his mind, heart, and soul.

After a bit we turned and looked down on our party around a now cheery little fire. In the eerie moonlight they lost individuality save in height and width and looked like a band of gypsies, some in skirts, some in trousers, all chattering, all moving.

"They look like *our* gypsies," whispered Malcolm, "the ones that camp each summer in the vacant lot and steal our chickens."

"Yes." And I snickered, "And roast our chickens on spits, and when Papa smells them so delicious how he roars and rages and stamps his foot."

"What a noise they make down there with their gabbling," my brother said, "The sea has a so much nicer voice."

We went down the cliff, skirted the periphery of the group, and found a secluded spot apart where we could watch and not miss anything.

"We're safe here," I said. "The saps won't find us; the elders think we should sit with them because they are the right age for us, not realizing they are the wrong everything else."

"They are absolutely sickening," he agreed.

Two milking goats doing agitated cud work lay down close to our flanks, so we had congenial company. No one saw us and we had a box-seat view.

"Look. James and Michael are laying horse blankets now around the fire — eating time must be getting close," I said. Then, "Listen," as Mama's and Aunt Maud's voices arose shrilly.

"If you boys" — addressing Uncle Mort and Papa — "think we are going to *sprawl* there to enjoy our oysters, suppose you both try on a corset of jabbing whalebones and while you're in them have a bout with this ghastly Paris fashion of jabots, where little whalebones threaten the jugular vein!"

We both laughed. "Wouldn't you know it," said Malcolm. "Professor Taussig, the peacemaker, is hightailing it for chairs."

"People really don't need to talk," I said, meditating, "to show themselves up. Look at Mary and Bridget pushing those great covered pans of oysters into the embers; their faces are all crinkled up and wrinkled in the firelight just like oysters. And Professor James is sitting clasping his knees and gazing into the fire and I bet he doesn't even know he's on a picnic."

"Jeepers," said Malcolm. "Look at Matthew Macy, his foot on the step of the victoria, leaning forward talking to Aunt Fanny, and see Uncle Mort way off watching him like a lynx. I bet he's drooling to join them but is afraid he'll get 'bit' again. By gum, he's going to try it, he's creeping up there slow and easy."

"He's there now. See Matthew Macy straighten up and show his teeth — I can't tell with all that foliage on his face and not seeing his eyes whether he's smiling or about to attack. Lorks! Aunt Fanny is taking Uncle Mort's hand and is laying it against her cheek and now Matthew Macy has covered up his teeth again and they are all talking together nice as pie."

Malcolm nudged me and said, "You'd better 'miaow' when Cassie passes us. We're kind of in shadow and your miaow is the only thing you do better than me."

"Indeed, and when you try to bray like a donkey you sound like the ferry *Gay Head* coming around Brant Point," I snapped.

"You're getting hungry, little sister. It always makes you cross. There go Cassie and about five others with plates of food — miaow, I tell you."

I miaowed and Cassie winked at us. Soon she had us eating with gusto until we could hold no more.

When everyone had finished, a blessed lull, a sort of pensiveness, pervaded. Moonlight is cold, I decided, both to look at and to sense in one's bones. We pulled ourselves over on the blankets, the victoria was drawn closer to the fire, to which more faggots were added, and Mama and Aunt Maud got in with Aunt Fanny and turned up their golf cape collars. The men lit cigars with long twigs from the fire. Professor James's eyes never left the Hermit's face; they had a questioning expression in them.

An answering look brought the Hermit to his feet and all eyes were upon him. He looked around at everyone and then said and his voice had sadness in it, "Professor James's European friend sent him words of affection which I never expected to have an opportunity to deliver. I was with him when he studied with Hatha Yogi in the high Himalayas."

The group started to withdraw then, but the Hermit put up a protesting hand and they sat back. He also sat down.

"It may well be," he continued, "that this truly miraculous meeting may mean the time of disclosure has come, for in order to tell of Professor James's friend I have to preface it by how I came to meet him.

"You have heard of the horrors of the Australian colonization, where criminals transported from British jails by evil ship captains and evil landowners were used as slave labor and illicit money was exchanged for that purpose. Happening to be on a dock in Liverpool one night, I was seized, gagged, and shanghaied as one of these unfortunates. I will not dwell on the tortures, starvation we endured, or the terror with which the end was anticipated by us — for we wretches were to be thrown to the sharks which are very plentiful off the coast of Australia, so that all traces of the illegal traffic might be erased. This was regularly done by the inhuman brutes when we could no longer toil for them. If the ladies will pardon me —."

Here he drew up his trouser legs, showing deep, serrated scars about each ankle. "The chains and manacles were put on continually, regardless of the condition of the wounds. Only the salt water and constant bleeding saved us from lockjaw. Also probably the searing of hot embers, for it amused the drunken overseer to toss burning bits of the faggots from the fire into the raw surfaces of our wounds and hear the screams of agony. After our meager supper cooked on this fire we were herded into a one-room jailhouse and locked in to sleep on the hard, bare floor.

"One dark night our overseer was so drunk he did not notice that I was behind him, and that was how I escaped. All night I traveled toward the mountains, and just before dawn stumbled over the freshly killed carcass of a kangaroo, partially torn apart and eaten. I too ate of it.

"I was now in underbrush almost waist-high and, knowing that I would be followed as a possible tale-bearer of their illicit traffic and foreseeing the fearful death that would await me, I searched my mind frantically for a possible escape from the brutal overseer. The kangaroo, some seven feet in length and already skinned in part, could make a disguise for me, I figured, and I went at finishing the skinning with sharp stones and sticks.

"The large ears and small head serving as a sort of crude cap, the hide draped over my body, I could proceed in leaps and possibly avoid detection, as kangaroos are very plentiful in Australian spaces and they would excite no interest. I must find water — and soon — if I were to survive, and if I could reach the mountain slopes I would find shepherds and their flocks. I think it was the fear and horror of that dorsal fin turning over for the attack that made me go on, for I had no interest left in life, my soul was rotted with hatred and bitterness.

"I reached the mountain slopes half dead and was taken by a kindly shepherd into his hut and fed and rested. After months — it may have been years, for I lost track of time — I heard of the yogis in the high Himalayas."

He paused here and gazed into the fire, which was burning down but giving heat. Then he went on.

"I knew I could not get back from the beast I had become to man again, alone. Like this fire, in order to keep burning, an outside force must feed it. There must have been a spark of desire left in me, for I journeyed long and far to find these holy men.

"And now, Professor James, we come to your European friend and the messages of love and affection he sent you in case I should ever meet you in America, should I return. With his help and interest I went through with Hatha Yogi the fasting from food and sleep, the breathing exercises and the trials of self-discipline from which he got strength of will and deeper moral and intellectual powers and from which I got *nothing* — save a deepening by physical deprivation of the bestial qualities already so deeply rooted. Your friend interested himself in my plight and understood my firm conviction that I could now do nothing for myself by myself. He said that in Frankfurt am Main was a new research hospital dealing with the subconscious mind, and thence he went with me, paying my way and telling to the doctors my story."

Here he paused and Uncle Mort quietly got up and drew close.

"I came out of the prophylactic institution where, under the supervision of your friend, Professor James, I had been subjected to scientific experiments of which I had no knowledge. I was possessed by an intense desire for my homeland and my benefactor seemed to be satisfied with my craving, calling it a first step in my rehabilitation. Pressing a purse into my hand, he bade me godspeed.

"Like a homing pigeon I came back here to the land of my birth and claimed my inheritance of this land. In *rebirth*, Professor James, I found enlargement, as in *birth* the new life expands in the mother's womb. The solitude, ocean, sky, and moors nurtured me — in them I found my God."

The voice ceased. The Hermit sat looking up at the moon, his eyes were bright. This sudden silence must have awakened me from my reveries, for I sat up and rubbed my eyes. As if immured, the group around the fire sat gazing into it, not a word spoken. Had I been dreaming? Were the dreadful sharks and the kangaroo a nightmare?

On the periphery there was movement beginning. Lanterns were lit and fastened onto the wagons, horses were harnessed, brought out, and hooked up, the remains of the picnic supper were being packed up by the "girls" and put into the wagons, our ponies were led out and fastened on behind. Still the group sat on in silence, wrapped in thought, around the dying fire.

Matthew Macy, after a glance around at them, got up quietly and joined the others at the wagons. This roused Professor James and Professor Taussig, who followed him. Malcolm waked up and whispered, "Look, they're all hearing it again, without talking. Jeepers, what a story Matthew Macy told!" I looked around.

Papa had risen and was walking up and down, his hands behind his back; Uncle Mort was watching him. Aunt Fanny was wiping tears away, Mama and Aunt Maud, arm in arm, were walking toward the cliff.

"By gum," said my brother, "look at my godfather — he's been on the cliff the whole time with his telescope, never heard a word."

"It's all over," I said to Malcolm sadly, "the great Harvest Moon Celebration, the fire's nearly out, the moon's under a cloud, summer's over, they'll all be leaving tomorrow. It's *all, all* over."

As they left us next day and went through the turnstile on the way to the ferry, Professor James turned for a last wave to my parents on the piazza and called out, "This really has been a great experience. Mrs. Howe shall hear of Mr. Macy's tale, I assure you. We're leaving with much more than we came with, Harold and Alice — heartfelt thanks for this memorable visit."

Malcolm was right. It wasn't an ending, especially for Papa, who ever since the night before had been strangely detached. When my brother asked him about a puzzling lecture on logic Mrs. Richard Cabot gave at his school that next winter, in which she had said, "One way to prove the right direction to a given point is to take the wrong one," and then took the class straight into a course on ethics, Malcolm asked, "Papa, is that true too in ethics?" And Papa replied and looked so sad, "I'm afraid so, oftentimes."

On Uncle Mort's door at the Medical School, myopic as he was, he could not but see the new words under "Morton Prince, M.D., Psychology" — "Lectures on Hypnotic Suggestion, Thursdays 2 P.M." Summoning Uncle Mort into his office, Papa explained the sign.

"How often my puritanical bigotry has made me draw wrong inferences, Mort — like the attitude I had toward hypnotism. I confess it now wholeheartedly. Without hypnotism old Jethro would have died of lockjaw, Matthew Macy would probably never have been rehabilitated, your girl of the bells never made normal again. Surely a few misapplications by charlatans could never offset the multiple benefits."

Papa got up. "Can I come to one of your lectures, Mort?"

Uncle Mort hugged him. "Of course, you old reprobate," and they both laughed.